CHANGING THE WORLD

Finding Your Place in the Great Commission

Pastor Darrel Deuel
Executive Director, The Sending Place

John W. Drebinger Jr., C.Ht., CSP
Certified Speaking Professional

First Edition

**Wulamoc Publishing,
Galt, California**

Changing The World
Finding Your Place in the Great Commission

By Darrel Deuel and
John Warner Drebinger Jr., C.Ht., CSP

Published by:
Wulamoc Publishing
Post Office Box 1406
Galt, CA 95632-1406 U.S.A.

Copyright © 2005
by Darrel Deuel and John W. Drebinger Jr.
First Printing 2005
Printed in the United States of America
Cover design by Ad Graphics, Tulsa, Oklahoma
Phone: (800) 368-6196

Deuel, Darrel and Drebinger, John W., Jr.
CHANGING THE WORLD: Finding Your Place in the Great Commission
by Darrel Deuel and John Warner Drebinger Jr. 1st ed.
Includes bibliographical references.
ISBN 1-890296-04-X (pbk.)

Order Information

To order additional copies of this book or to receive information.

Contact:
The Sending Place
PO Box 730
Elk Grove, CA 95759

Phone:
(877) 3-SENDING
(877) 373-6346
(916) 685-2331

Visit Our Website:

http://www.thesendingplace.com

E-Mail:

director@thesendingplace.com

Warning - Disclaimer

This book is designed to provide information on missions and *The Sending Place*™. It is sold with the understanding that the publisher and author are not engaged in rendering legal, accounting, or other professional services. Also, the authors, while experts in teaching and training people to serve in missions, are not able to know your particular circumstances. If legal or other expert assistance is required, the services of a competent professional should be sought.

It is not the purpose of this book to reprint all the information that is otherwise available to the authors and/or publisher, but to complement, amplify, and supplement other texts. You are urged to read all the available material, learn as much as possible about missions, and to tailor the information to your individual needs. For more information, see the many references in the recommended reading list.

Missions and the organizations that sponsor them are many and varied. You should investigate whichever ones you choose with which to affiliate. This book is in no way an endorsement of the performance, safety, or correct theology of any given mission effort.

Every effort has been made to make this book as complete and accurate as possible. However, there **may be mistakes,** both typographical and in content. Therefore, this text should be used only as a general guide and not as the ultimate source of information on this subject. Furthermore, this book contains information on missions only up to the printing date.

The purpose of this book is to educate and entertain. The authors and Wulamoc Publishing shall have neither liability nor responsibility to any person or entity with respect to any loss or damage caused, or alleged to be caused, directly or indirectly by the information contained in this book.

If you do not wish to be bound by the above, you may return this book to the publisher for a full refund.

Acknowledgments

John Drebinger

One of the special privileges of writing a book is that you get to publicly thank people who have had a profound effect on your life. This is where I get to thank some of the people who have helped me on my journey. For the average reader, these people may be unknown, but I wish you had the opportunity to enjoy the pleasure of knowing them as I have over the years.

First, I am grateful to God for the direction He has given me in life and to the outstanding model teacher, Jesus, who in addition to giving his life for me, also showed me and the world how to teach and communicate most effectively. Pastors of the churches I have attended over the years, Fred Doty, Robert Blacka, Luther Tolo, Vern Holmes, Charlie Knorr, Scott Minke, Tim Stevenson, Darrel Deuel, Richard Eddy, Robert Salge, Len Brokenshire, and Steve Lundblom. Their teachings have planted many seeds, which have developed into the ideas I share with others today. To Steve and Karen Oeffling who are outstanding models of service and ministry. Bruce Wilkinson CSP, who introduced me to the National Speakers Association and allowed me to use one of his stories.

Next, my Mom and Dad, Bernadette and John Drebinger, for giving me life and always being there to help and guide me. My wonderful wife, Karen, who has stood beside me for the past 34 years of marriage and always been there when I needed her. My children, Jessica and Johnny, for being the best kids I could have ever hoped for.

Sandie Gilbert, my editor, who on many occasions worked late into the night in order to make me appear to be literate.

Darrel Deuel

I would like to acknowledge those who have had a major impact on my life, and my life's direction. That begins with my incredible heavenly Father, who created me for a purpose, and called me to His work early in my life, and to His precious Son, our Lord and Savior Jesus Christ, for His constant forgiveness of me and my imperfections, and to the Holy Spirit, who keeps pointing me toward Jesus, and who empowers me to do the tasks He calls me to do.

I thank my father and mother, Francis and Elina Deuel, and my sister, Deanna Lesku, for the loving, grace-filled family environment I grew up in. I thank my wife, Janet, and children Jamie, Dan, and Darren, for their great help and support to me, and for their great patience over the years, even when I have been away from home too much.

I acknowledge two men who were great mentors to me, embodying the excellent qualities of being a pastor, Walter Nordby and Gordon Selbo. The members of St. Timothy's Lutheran Church in San Jose, California, and St. Peter's Lutheran Church in Elk Grove, California, for their love and support during the 30 years I served them.

I appreciate the excellent work of all those pastors who were my associates and friends over the years, Todd Mattson, Dan Selbo, Arnold Vocke, Rich Eddy, Joel Midthun, and Robert Salge.

A special thanks to John Drebinger, whose positive spirit and expertise helped greatly in putting this book together. Thanks to *The Sending Place*™ Board of Directors for their faithful work in sharing the vision of getting the ministry rolling: Janet Deuel, John Drebinger Jr., Ralph Feaster, Pastor Bill Moberly, Diana Oldfield, Pastor Dan Selbo, Bill Wittich and Mike Yount.

Thanks to the many, many people who are responding to God's call to "Go and make disciples of all nations." Because of their faithful work, God's Word is going out "...to the ends of the earth."

We would both like to thank, Nita Hanson, Steve Oeffling, Tim Stevenson, Maureen Feaster, Janet Deuel, Paul Holte, Scott Geller, Naomi Rhode, Glenna Salsbury, and Edward A. Wescott, Jr., for their help in making this work effective in serving God.

Dedication

We dedicate this to the many faithful followers of Jesus who become "Goers" or "Senders".

Table Of Contents

Chapter Contents Preview

CHAPTER ONE: How To Use This Book
- Write Down Your Ideas, Questions, and Commitments
- Questions Can Be Your Compass
- Reading This Book Effectively

CHAPTER TWO: Good News: You Don't Have to Go!
- Is Ministry For God Or For Us?
- Which Is Easier, Doing It Yourself or With Your Child?

CHAPTER THREE: Put Your Problems In Perspective
- Put Your Problems In Perspective
- Earthly Challenges
- God's Perspective
- Opportunities For Growth
- Making Problems Look Small
- Which Way Should We Focus?
- The Great Commission
- Achieving Godly Goals
- Messengers From Far Away Have Great Impact
- What Impact Are You Having?
- Sending – A Larger Perspective

CHAPTER FOUR: Trivial Pursuit or Meaningful Purpose?
- Trivial Pursuit
- A Life of Meaningful Purpose
- Beginning the Journey
- *The Sending Place*™ Vision

CHAPTER FIVE: This Could Be You!
- Possible Mission Teams
- Petrozavodsk, Russia
- Kisumu, Kenya
- Johannesburg, South Africa
- Guatemala City, Guatemala
- Bila Tserkva, Ukraine

CHAPTER TEN: Reasons Why You Think You Can't Go

- Reasons You Can't Go and How God Can Overcome Them
- I Don't Have the Time
- I Met A Missionary Once
- My Church Supports (The national church body)
- I'm Afraid To Fly
- Let The Pros Do It
- Our Youth Go to Mexico Every Year
- I Would Have Done That When I Was Younger, But I'm Retired Now
- I Can't Afford It, and I Can't Ask Others for Money
- My Children Are Too Young
- We Have So Many Programs In Our Church Right Now, We Just Don't Have Time For Any More
- We're Doing A Big Building Project Right Now, And Cannot Afford To Do Anything Else
- We're Already Supporting Several Missionaries
- We Support (Some Other Agency)
- We Just Want To Ease Into Missions. Maybe We'll Call You Later
- I Know of Another Group Doing Mission Work. Why Don't You Contact Them?
- Some Concluding Thoughts

CHAPTER ELEVEN: What We Have Left Undone

- What We Have Left Undone
- We Have Left the Biggest Thing of All Undone
- The Greatest Mission Activity of All Time is Now
- Are You Ready?

CHAPTER TWELVE: God Is A Missionary God

- God Called His People To Go From The Beginning
- The Great Commission
- Today Is An Exciting Time

CHAPTER THIRTEEN: What Is My Next Step?

- Take Action

CHAPTER THIRTEEN: What Is My Next Step? (Continued)

- Get Some Training
- Read All Training Materials
- Become A Sender
- Involve Your Home Congregation
- Report To Your Congregation

Introduction

You are about to discover one of the most exciting opportunities in which God allows us to participate. Up until now, you knew missions existed, and you probably believed they were important for someone else to carry out. But what is your part in this adventure in distant lands? Sending? Going? Or both?

We are living in exciting times! Change is the only thing that seems to be constant. The world is changing, and God's people are changing their approach to better serve Him and His people. If you live in any larger city or suburban area, you have seen churches spring up in shopping malls and in buildings that are not part of the traditional model. Many churches have discovered they can get more for their dollar by moving into existing structures or leasing until they can afford to build a bigger building. This has caused us to look at church property and buildings differently than we have before.

Mission work has changed as well. More and more people are becoming interested in serving God by entering the mission field. To accommodate them, a new field of missions has developed. We will refer to it as "short-term missions." These shorter missions extending from a couple of weeks to a few months have allowed many more of God's people to serve Him and respond to his command to proclaim Jesus as Lord to the ends of the earth. Speaking locally and around the country, we hear over and over again, "I didn't know this type of mission and this type of training opportunity existed." Well, the good news is that it does, and we are here to help you find your place in the Great Commission.

We want you to discover God's purpose for you when it comes to fulfilling His Great Commission to preach the Gospel to all nations!

The Great Commission is from Matthew 28:19 where Jesus tells His followers to "Go therefore and make disciples of all nations." There is no question we are called to be involved. The question for many is how?

The authors of this book have varied backgrounds. Darrel Deuel has served as a pastor in the Lutheran Church for over 30 years. He felt called to ensure Christians would be actively involved in missions around the world. He also learned the value of training people before they go on a mission. Training is one of the unique parts of *The Sending Place's* ™ approach to missions.

Pastor Deuel's coauthor, John Drebinger, is a professional speaker and for the past 14 years has been teaching communication skills to most of the top corporations in the United States. He brings to this work a layman's view and a look at missions from the viewpoint of someone new to the field. While attending his first board of directors meeting for *The Sending Place*™, he realized the need for Pastor Deuel and *The Sending Place*™ to have a book to tell their story and share with you information which cannot be conveyed in a short sermon on missions. John proposed he and Darrel write the book together. John's experience as an author and publisher led to the creation of this book.

For those of you who notice grammar and capitalization, you will probably notice as our editor did that we have chosen not to capitalize "satan" even though it is a proper noun. Since we always capitalize God and any reference to Him, we do not want to show the same level of respect to the prince of darkness.

To make the book easier to read we will use the word "we" rather than I throughout the book. If it is significant we will mention who a particular story is about.

We hope this book is a step along your journey to the discovery of the exciting life God has in store for you. When you have finished this book, please consider joining us by contacting us in person. We look forward to talking with you in the future and we are always available by email at director@thesendingplace.com or john@drebinger.com

May God bless you as you invest the time to read this book and may He guide you along the path He wants you to walk.

Chapter 1

How To Use This Book

"Committing your thoughts to print creates a void in your mind which your creative spirit will fill with new ideas"

-- John W. Drebinger Jr.

"Writing down your ideas, questions, and commitments is like planting them in fertile soil."
- John W. Drebinger Jr.

Write Down Your Ideas, Questions, and Commitments
        John writes: While reading a book written by a friend of mine, I found that as I read it I was coming up with all sorts of ideas I could use in my speaking career. I happened to be on a short commuter flight and didn't have my laptop computer out for taking notes and had no paper with me. I know from experience that if I think of a good idea and fail to write it down, I will forget it. Also, if God begins leading me I need to write down the action to which I am committed. While on the plane, I took out my pen and proceeded to write in the space on the inside of the front and back covers as well as several partially blank pages of the book with my notes. Once home, I transferred these ideas to the journal in my computer. Had I not gone to the effort of writing them down, several ideas included in this book would have been lost.
        You may have experienced talking with someone when you thought of something and sure enough, later in the day you struggled with, "What was it that occurred to me earlier?" It is so easy to read Scripture or any book and have God reveal to you a direction in which you are to go, only to have satan use the clutter of the day and the busy nature of your life to bury it deep in your unconscious mind. Losing ideas or direction can be a hindrance to achieving all God has in store for us.
        Because your mind works this way, we have provided a section in the back of this book where you can record your inspirations from God. Writing them down allows you the freedom to return to them for deeper consideration, prayer, and taking action. If you record them on a separate piece of paper, we recommend you also write them into the book as they will always be where you may refer to them. This way, the book becomes more valuable to you each time you pick it up and add more thoughts.

You won't want to lend your notated copy to a friend so you will just have to buy another one from us. All kidding aside, with the notes recorded, you will always know where to find them.

Questions Can Be Your Compass

The direction your thinking takes is quite often directed by whatever question you are attempting to answer at the moment. Questions may give either positive or negative direction to your life. Questions contain a bias which will affect the answers you get. The questions we ask direct the results we achieve so it is important to design the questions you ask yourself to ensure a positive result. For example, if you ask, "Why can't I participate in missions?" You will end up with a list like:

- I don't have the time.
- I don't have the money.
- I don't know what to do.

If you ask, "What do I have to do to either go on a mission or send someone else?" You will get a more resourceful list that will be solution oriented. On occasion, you might get stuck and not be able to come up with an answer. The basic technique in dealing with this is to respond with the following question or a slight variation thereof.

"I know I don't know _____, but if I did know what would it (or they) be."

For example, consider the above question, What do I have to do to either go on a mission or send someone else? If you were stuck, you would ask yourself, "I know I don't know what I have to do but if I did know what would it be?" This simple technique will allow you to discover the solutions rather than the obstacles.

If you are aware that questions direct and help how you think, it would be a good idea to make effective use of them when writing and reading a book. When we began to write this book, we had to ask ourselves, "What is our purpose in writing this book?" Some of the answers we discovered were:

- To give glory to God.
- To share with others the ministry of *The Sending Place*™.
- To help people discover how they can better serve God and fulfill the Great Commission.
- To be able to provide people with more information than any brochure could cover about how to become involved.
- To reach people for Christ around the world.
- To strengthen local churches by expanding their vision.

The next question that directed our writing was, "What is the desired outcome the book should achieve for the reader?"

- To give you, the reader, a desire to become a part of God's work in missions.
- To help you discover if you are a goer, sender, or pretender.
- To guide you on the first steps to being involved and taking action.

Reading This Book Effectively

For years, educators and reading comprehension experts have said that students should read the review questions at the end of each chapter before reading the chapter in order to get the most out of it. If this is really effective, and we believe it is, then why not put the questions at the front of each chapter? So, in order to increase comprehension, we have taken two steps you might find helpful. First, prior to the "Introduction" there is a section titled, "Chapter Contents Preview" (page 15).

Its purpose is to alert your mind to the topics covered in the entire book and in each chapter. If you haven't read this already, please take a moment and do so now. The second step is a set of questions at the beginning of each chapter. Read these prior to reading that chapter. The following question is repeated with each chapter because it is designed to help you discover God's desire for you. "What is my place in the Great Commission? We know you don't know what your place is but if you did know what would it be?

We will let you in on a secret as you read some of these questions. They will have words in them that have not been defined in the context of this subject. This is done intentionally, as it will cause your mind to be slightly confused and evoke a state of searching for the answers.

As you read and discover answers to the above questions, quickly write them down in the back of the book. When you are done reading, review your ideas and then write down actions you can take immediately which will start the ball rolling.

"Expect great things from God. Attempt great things for God."

-William Carey

Chapter 2

Good News: You Don't Have to Go!

"It's one of the greatest joys of a short-term mission—seeing God break down barriers that separate us. We get to taste what heaven will be like—to know hints of the joy of Pentecost, to glimpse our gathering before the throne of God."

-- J. Mack and Leeann Stiles

Questions To Enhance Your Reading

1. What is my place in the Great Commission?

2. Who is responsible for ministry?

3. Who benefits most from missions, the senders, the goers, or those being ministered to?

4. What is the difference between "having" to do something and "getting" to do something?

"God doesn't need you to reach the world for Christ. He can do it on His own, but why would you want to miss out on the joy?"

- John W. Drebinger Jr.

Is Ministry for God or for Us?

Let's face it--does the all-powerful God of the universe need you and me to get his message across? After all, He could just write it across the sky or on the mountain tops. He could send an angel to every living person with the message of salvation and a personal invitation. We, along with you could think of hundreds of ways an infinite God could get His message out, yet He chose to use us. Why? That is a good question. We believe it was because He didn't want to keep all the joy, and the wonder to Himself.

Even from the very beginning, God has chosen to make us part of His plan to provide salvation for His lost children. In the Garden of Eden, God laid out the plan and provided that a Savior would be born to a woman. He clearly didn't have to involve us; especially in light of how we so quickly made a mess of the perfect world He created and into which we were placed. Think of how God used men and women throughout the Old Testament to set the stage for the advent of the Messiah.

We believe there are several reasons He chose to involve us. Other writers in the field of missions have shared many of them. For us, it seems that God, our loving Father, wanted to continue His relationship with us, and as the perfect father he did it by involving us. Once again, did He need us? No!

Which Is Easier, Doing It Yourself or With Your Child?

What similarities can you think of in your life? If you have children, you can relate to this example. As children grow up they show an interest in participating in what Mom and Dad are doing. If you are working in the yard, they want to "help". Do you let them because it will make the work go faster? Probably not, in fact with little children, involving them usually takes a great deal more effort than doing it alone. But a loving parent gets out a small rake or tool and lets them work along with them. We also think there is a great lesson here for us. If we don't let our kids help when they really can't, it is unlikely they will help when they can. We build the connection with them helping by making them a part of our life early on.

When a child wants to help in the kitchen, another opportunity occurs for the project to take longer and make a bigger mess, but the joy of doing it together and what it does for the child is very valuable. We think it is the same in our relationship with God. When He lets us get involved in His plans, it certainly complicates His existence, but He allows us to partake with Him because He knows how valuable it is for our growth and continued relationship with Him.

What we should strive for is the same attitude a child has wanting to "work" with Mom or Dad. We should be anxious to help out and just be with our loving Heavenly Father, just as our children crave our attention and want to be with us. Unlike many earthly parents, who don't take time or have time to spend with their kids, our Father in Heaven has an infinite amount of time for us. We just need to want to spend our time with Him. We want to spend time with Him, not to earn His love, but as a response to His love for us.

As for the title of this chapter, "Good News: You Don't Have To Go!" what we had in mind is that we over use the phrase, "have to." There is precious little that we "have to" or "must" do in life. Also, almost anything in life you "have to do" isn't enjoyable. We guarantee you that no kid has ever said, "I have to go to Disneyland." They tell their friends how they "get to" go to Disneyland. Once again, we need to remember we are God's children and perhaps we need to behave more like children when it comes to enthusiasm about spending time with our Father doing His work and His will. So, when it comes to preaching the Gospel to the world we don't "have to." God lets us participate with him. Remember, you "get to" take part in the greatest work anyone of us can do in service to God and our earthly brothers and sisters! We hope this book helps you better understand your place in God's vineyard.

Chapter 3

Put Your Problems In Perspective

"The difficulty or challenge of a problem is gauged by your viewpoint. Looking at it from our perspective, it may appear overwhelming, but from God's perspective it's much smaller and achievable."
-- John W. Drebinger Jr.

Questions To Enhance Your Reading

1. What is my place in the Great Commission?

2. Do my personal problems often distract me from doing God's work?

3. How big or small is my own personal world on which I focus?

4. What impact am I having on the world on behalf of Jesus Christ?

PUT YOUR PROBLEMS IN PERSPECTIVE

If choosing the best perspective can empower you and your life, then what perspective would be absolutely the most empowering? God's perspective, clearly, would be the best. He sees things for what they really are and no challenge is too great for Him to overcome. In fact, from God's perspective our challenges are merely lessons, or pathways that lead us to the best outcome available to us. We just can't always see it from our viewpoint. So how can we get God's perspective? One outstanding way is to join in on the work God gave us to do.

One of the greatest gifts God gives those who respond to His call to preach the Gospel to all nations is that we begin to experience God's perspective of our life and the challenges we face day to day. Each and every one of us has difficulties, problems, or as we choose to refer to them, challenges. A fascinating thing about challenges is that they are not absolute in their difficulty.

We have an enormous task in front of us, that is making sure at least someone from every group of people in the world will believe in Jesus and will be in the heavenly mansion. It is estimated that there are still over 8,000 people groups, (a group of people with ethnic identity), in this world who do not yet have a Christian church within the group.

Are you ready to finally help achieve this enormous task? Unfortunately, it's easy to quickly get distracted from the work at hand, easy to lose focus on what you are really to be about each day as a follower of Jesus Christ because there are many things that will try to get in the way.

Earthly Challenges

So let us begin by asking you to ponder for a moment. How are things going for you personally these days? We would imagine you are facing quite a variety of problems, which is quite normal for life in this fallen world!

Perhaps your life at school or work is somewhat less than wonderful. Is there someone you have to be around every day that is a real pain to you? Maybe you're fighting some sort of health problem. Perhaps you have some major health issues, or some aches and pains that are a real nuisance. Is your life filled with stress and tension? How are things going these days in your family? Are you always happy to see each other when you return home in the evening? If you're married, is your relationship healthy and strong, or are there some problems? And if you have children, are they kind, loving, and obedient? For you children, are your parents kind and loving to you? Or in your families are there tugs of war, and tension, and other problems going on? And how are things going these days in your congregation? Might there be a few difficulties going on right there?

Yes, it's not unusual to have problems in your personal life, problems at school and work, problems in your families, and even problems amongst a group of Christian people who are bound together in a congregation.

And yet, amidst all the problems we have in this life, we want to remind you that God wants you as a Christian to put your problems in perspective! Never dwell on your problems, never let them get you down, never let them win over you!

God's Perspective

That is easy to say, but how can we actually do it? God gives us many ways to put our problems in perspective. The reality is that He offers to view our problems from His perspective. After all, something that seems overwhelming to us has a whole different look when you examine it from an infinite, divine viewpoint.

God clearly expects us to grow during our lifetime. From our personal lives to business, we see that if we cease growing or learning we begin to die. The most vibrant people on the planet are dedicated to constantly growing and learning. God wishes us to grow in our spiritual strength and in our relationship with Him. The Holy Spirit gently moves us along our life's journey encouraging us to grow in our faith. We resist or accept the guidance, and if we accept it, we grow and our lives improve as does our relationship with God. Sadly, satan is able to immobilize many Christians to never grow beyond the point of their salvation. It certainly is a defeat to satan whenever someone comes to God through Christ, but what can he do to keep the loss to a minimum? He wants to prevent the growing and strengthening of each and every Christian.

Opportunities For Growth

One important aspect which helps us grow is the gathering together as a congregation of believers, which we are admonished to do in Hebrews 10:25, "...not neglecting to meet together, as is the habit of some, but encouraging one another."

Sharing one's faith is another great opportunity to grow in your faith. If you want to accelerate your growth, all you have to do is be open to God's leading, and follow His advice as we find it in His word, the Bible. When Jesus gave us the Great Commission in Matthew 28 to preach the Gospel to the nations, He showed us a path to incredible spiritual growth.

Once again, whenever God invites us to join Him in His work, it is for our benefit. After all, we know God is infinite, which means He is all-sufficient to accomplish anything He wishes, so why does He need us? It is so we can share in all that He has for us. The abundant life He promises us in John 10:10 doesn't begin when we die. Rather, it begins right here and now, as we follow our Savior.

Are we saying that when someone becomes a Christian that problems miraculously disappear from their life? Not at all. But again, God wants you to put your problems in the right perspective. As we might expect, God has a very unique way of doing that!

Making Problems Look Small

Indeed, His approach is not to take the problems away. He just makes them "look" small! How does he make them "look" small? By enlightening us with His perspective. You see, that's what we learn from the prophet Isaiah in the 49th chapter of his book. Here, the servant is speaking, and he is complaining about his problems.

He has been working hard for the Lord in his home area, but does not seem to be bearing much fruit. He is frustrated because all his work from his perspective appears to amount to nothing. The local people are not responding.

The great things the servant wants to have happen locally are not happening. He's feeling down in the dumps. He's worked hard, but it's looking like it was a waste of time. Do you ever feel that way? You've tried your best to do God's work but you just seem to be hitting a brick wall that you can't break through.

So what does God do? God tells him in verse six, "It is too light a thing that you should be my servant to raise up the tribes of Jacob and to restore the preserved of Israel; I will give you as a light to the nations, that my salvation may reach to the end of the earth." Notice how God does not take away any of the servant's problems, He doesn't try to make him feel good by patting him on the back and saying, "Nice try anyway."

Wow, isn't that amazing? Do you see what God just did, and what He keeps doing today? When the servant concludes he's worked as hard as he can, and accomplished all that he can where he is, that he might as well retire, God says his work has just been too small anyway! The servant was looking at things from his own perspective and they looked too big. God knew this and gave him a greater task which would also give him a Godly perspective realizing that he couldn't do it on his own and reminded him of something that we all need to remember, that all things are possible with God. We just need to be doing God's work in order to see God make the impossible not only possible, but easy.

No longer should the servant focus just on his own life or his work in the local area. From now on he should go to the nations, to make sure God's plan of salvation reaches to the ends of the earth! This is the purpose God has for those of us who are followers of Jesus Christ. He wants our main focus to be on proclaiming His glory to the ends of the earth!

Which Way Should We Focus?

We strongly believe that American Christians must take this far more seriously! We dare not keep our main focus centered on the wants and needs of our own family or congregation!

Have you ever noticed that churches that are inwardly focused seem to have more problems than those who are doing ministry on a larger scale? First, this is because God knew what He was doing when He commanded us to reach out to the world. Churches that are inwardly focused see the budget from a different viewpoint. The visionary budget seems impossible because their viewpoint is too small. When they see that their true mission is reaching the world, they realize God expects an even bigger budget. They also realize when taking on a larger project that they can't do it on their own. They must have God's help to raise the funds and get the task done. When they raise a budget worthy of God's bigger projects, the money for the smaller ones either is found or the need for the smaller project disappears. Either way, we win.

We dare not keep our main focus on doing ministry in just our own community or state or country. If we do, we shift from God's global perspective to our own small, local perspective, taking God's great commission and making it humanly possible to do on a small scale. Now that we have made it something we can imagine succeeding at, we make a further mistake by beginning to rely on ourselves and not God. A huge advantage of keeping on track with God's huge goals and tasks is that we must rely on Him in order to get it done. God made it very clear to His people 2,700 years ago with Isaiah, and even before that, that our main task is always to be "a light to the nations"! This is a Godly task in which He wants us to take part. He doesn't expect us to do it without Him, rather He wants to share the joy of the task with us.

The Great Commission

Jesus also reminded us of this task when He walked on the earth. The Great Commission of Matthew 28 gives us no options except to, "Go, and make disciples of all nations!"

These passages have certainly changed Darrel Deuel's life personally. They are what led him to resign his twenty-three year call as Senior Pastor of St. Peter's Lutheran Church in Elk Grove, California, to become full-time Director of *The Sending Place*™, a Missionary Training Center. The concept of developing a new missionary training center was a huge task, one which Pastor Deuel, the board of directors, trainers, missionaries, and senders (donors) could not do on their own. God has us rely on Him, and uses us as His church to support each other. We must rely on God to lead people like you to seek and save the lost to join with us on this task.

The more others understand what God wants us to focus on, the more others are partnering with us to help save the lost around the world.

As with any congregation, the church you belong to has probably had its own struggles over the years. You've wanted your church to grow even more than it has. You want more people to come and worship the Lord with you, and serve the Lord with you, and study His word with you. But growth has sometimes been slower than you'd like.

God's way of making that problem look small is to tell you to look way beyond this community, and start focusing on His desire to save the lost all over the world!

Achieving Godly Goals

John Drebinger writes, I was once told by someone that in order to reach a goal you have to actually shoot past it. In my field of safety, many companies aiming for zero lost time injuries get stuck and can't seem to achieve that goal. The ones who have successfully reached zero actually focused on achieving a greater goal, and that is to achieve zero recordable injuries. By going after a greater goal, the other goal is much more likely to be attained.

It seems that focusing mission work on the local neighborhoods around your congregation is a worthy goal. It certainly pleases God and increases your church and its service. The problem is that by settling for a smaller goal or target we miss out on the stretching God can do in our life. In fact, by expanding our vision, we find that much is easy to do that we couldn't do before.

For those of you who remember when the United States took on the goal of landing a man on the moon and successfully returning him to earth, you saw what aiming for a huge goal can do. The changes to our life that have occurred due to the moon project have been incredible. The computer we are writing this book on is a product of the miniaturization that it took to build a spacecraft that could accomplish landing on the moon. Medical advances and many other achievements resulted from this endeavor. We wonder how long it would have taken to develop computers if the necessity for them had not been tied to a larger goal. The need to do very complex calculations resulted in the development of the computer. Calculators, and many other secondary advances, such as digital cameras with small memory cards have furthered the advances created by the space program.

Consistently, we find that the wisdom of God transcends the spiritual world and the same truths apply to every aspect of our existence.

When John had the experience of sharing the Gospel back in college with Campus Crusade for Christ, going to the beach and witnessing made sharing with fellow students on the college campus much easier. In a sense, God stretched his spiritual muscles and strengthened him so that when he was back in his own environment the task was easier.

Messengers From Far Away Have Great Impact

Darrel has discovered in his travels that there is often far more eagerness to hear the Gospel overseas than there is here at home! For example, he and his wife worked together doing mission work in South Africa. While they were there, they helped start 2 new churches! One of those churches was in the little village of Phaweni, way out in the bush. Darrel and Janet started by working with about 50 children in that village and then adults began to participate. They also had revival-type worship services for all ages every night for a week before the first Sunday service.

And you know what? When the mission team arrived in the village, there was not much to see. Very few people were out, as they drove the few blocks on dirt streets to our meeting place. But somehow, word got around fast! As the team arrived at the meeting place, they would look up the streets, and children were running as fast as they could to get to the team! By the time they got out of the van, they were surrounded by 20 or 30 children, with more on the way, eager to listen to more about Jesus!

Perhaps God used the uniqueness of visitors from another country, culture, or race to help attract people to hear His word. Even Jesus said in Mark 6:4, "A prophet is not without honor, except in his own country, and among his own kin, and in his own house." If Jesus discovered that a speaker from out of town had more weight than a local, why would we expect it to be different?

Once, when John was speaking to a corporation, he and the CEO of the company were walking down the hallway when the CEO said, "I have been telling them exactly what you told them for years, but they will do it because you said it." As an outside expert, John gave validation to his comments. The fact is, that from Jesus' time until now, outside experts have always carried more weight than someone from within the group. This is apparent if we look at the ministries of the early church. Paul traveled throughout the world and had a huge impact. The question we have for you is, who in the world would hear the message of the Gospel because you as a visitor from another nation shared it with them? They may just be waiting for you to arrive to hear the message of salvation. When will you go?

Darrel says, "I've got to tell you, I have never seen the kind of enthusiasm the African children had when I arrive to speak at many churches in North America!"

God really has prepared the hearts of people all over the world to hear His word now! But He needs more of us to go as His laborers in the harvest.

In fact, He is calling some of you who are reading this book! The Lord needs some of you to go with the powerful Gospel, to get out of your pews and get onto the planes! Is He calling you?

What Impact Are You Having?

As part of your on-going reflection on your life and ministry, we believe you should be asking yourself some important questions: What have you, as an individual and as a congregation, done recently to be part of God's great mission activity that He is right now doing around the world?

Indeed, as we talk to missionaries and leaders of mission agencies around the world, there is unanimous agreement that God is right now doing the greatest mission activity of all time! We hope none of you want to just sit on the sidelines and ignore it, or watch someone else do it! This is no time to be a spectator in the kingdom of God!

Where have you gone and what have you done to get out of your comfort zone, in order to share Christ and His love? How many new churches have you helped plant recently? How many missionaries has your congregation sent out so far this year? How many are you planning to send out next year?

How many orphans have you helped overseas, whose lives are now better because of what you have done? How much money are you giving regularly to the specific task of missions, the training and sending of missionaries?

If you do not like any of your answers to those questions, then it's time to change your answers! It's time to turn loose more of your time and resources to accomplish the great things God wants you to be doing for His kingdom!

As you do that, make sure you remember the way in which God wants to make your problems here "look" small. Indeed, as you recognize that your main focus, your main reason for existence, is to proclaim Jesus Christ as the light to all the nations of the world, it really does make your problems here look relatively quite small!

Can you sense God calling you to partner with us at *The Sending Place*™, to focus on bringing that light of Jesus to the nations?

People who we have trained and sent on missions have found that God has been able to use them in His mission field on trips that last anywhere from ten days to three weeks. They discovered that the short term mission field is one where we can share in fulfilling the Great Commission in the context of the life we live today. If you're not able to go, then that means you are a sender of those who do go! You can support them with your money and prayers and encouragement.

There aren't many other options. We are either senders or goers. Paul was supported on his mission journeys not by the people he was preaching to, but by those who had already responded to the message. They sent him on his way to reach more and more people. They gave of their wealth to send someone to peoples throughout the world.

Sending – A Larger Perspective

It is also important to realize that sending people begins by preparing them for their mission. That is the purpose of *The Sending Place*™. God may be calling you to support this ministry to prepare people to perform at their best and to have a productive journey for their own growth. Money raised to support an individual is only a small portion of what it takes to make world missions possible. A common mistake made by many people is to support just this small portion, and then as a result the greater organization that makes the mission possible must cut back and so recruit and train fewer and fewer missionaries. Remember, if in fact, God is going to help you grow and stretch your comfort zone, the level of support you give should be significant. Just as you must step out in faith as you leave for a mission, you must step out in faith as you become someone who sends others on a mission. Give not out of your excess and trust God to provide for your needs and wants. In fact, one place in the Bible where we are encouraged to test God is in the third chapter of Malachi where we are told to test God by tithing and see the results with which He responds.

You can also donate money to *The Sending Place*™ itself, as we are in the process of raising millions of dollars to build a facility, where we can bring missionaries on site to train them before they go overseas! It's a great way to get big results from the money God has given you to use for His glory!

Make sure you are living your life, with your main focus on proclaiming God's saving word to the world, being a light to the nations, as God expects of you! As a sender you enter the mission field by enabling us to train others and to send them on their journey prepared for their great adventure.

While we have the privilege of working together, remember that giving glory to God by being faithful to Him is our main purpose of living! Let's partner together to bring the Lord's salvation to the ends of the earth! Believe me, no task you have is more important!

Chapter 4

Trivial Pursuit or Meaningful Purpose?

"So many people today merely exist while living a life filled only with trivia."

--Darrel Deuel

Questions To Enhance Your Reading

1. What is my place in the Great Commission?

2. What is the most significant thing I have done in my life?

3. How has my life given glory to God?

4. Based upon how I invest my time, what value do I place on things or people?

Trivial Pursuit

      Have you ever played the game called "Trivial Pursuit©"? For those of you who have not played it, it's a board game during which a number of players gather to see who knows the most trivial facts, figures, and names you could imagine. You have to love a game that has the honesty to admit it has no valuable purpose other than the fun of playing. For instance, you might be asked things like,
"What future U.S. President, ravaged by a ruptured disc and malaria, saw his weight drop to 125 pounds during World War II?" (John F. Kennedy) or "Whose diva career took off with a soulful 'America the Beautiful' at the 1989 NBA Finals?" (Mariah Carey) or "Who became the first lefty in baseball history to fan 20 batters in nine innings of one game?" (Randy Johnson)
      What good is accomplished through these games? Not much, other than fun, fellowship, and using some brain matter, which is at least better than being a couch potato. But as most games do, they have a point at which they are supposed to be over. Someone wins the game, then you get on with your life.
      Playing a game is one thing, but how many people live a life of trivial pursuit? I don't mean asking obscure questions, but doing that which will never make a difference. Too many Christians live a life with no purpose

in mind. So many people today merely exist while living a life filled only with trivia. How often have you felt like you were living a non-stop version of "Trivial Pursuit" in your daily life?

It is interesting that in and of themselves none of the trivial pursuits of daily life are evil. It's that they can, if not kept to a reasonable level, crowd out that which really makes a difference in God's Kingdom. It's fine to have your favorite sitcoms or be excited about who wins next year's Super Bowl, but are those the things in your life that bring you the most excitement? We can assure you that while Darrel enjoys the elements of a good hunt, it is only a recreation or break in his real passion. Even then, he sees the glory of God in the beauty of the outdoors. While John enjoys looking for the latest gadget at the local backpacking supply store, there comes a time when it's time to do something with a purpose. Sadly, some of us are more concerned about where we are going to have lunch after church, than about how we are going to give glory to God during worship. It's an easy trap into which to fall.

When we think of satan leading people astray, we often think of people caught up in something evil. We don't see that we are being immobilized by the trivial. We may guard against greed, anger, and other more violent expressions of worldliness only to fall prey to the seemingly innocent. Many people on this earth really are living a non-stop version of "Trivial Pursuit." Unknowingly, lots of Christians get tied up in that kind of life, as well.

A Life of Meaningful Purpose

So how do we protect ourselves from being drawn into this trivial pursuit lifestyle, or how do we extricate ourselves if we find we are already living there? The best way is to live a life of purpose. When you have a purpose to your life, it is easier to stay on track. When we began writing this book, we first recorded our purpose for which it was being written. Why were we investing our lives and our money in publishing this book? Knowing our purpose allowed us to keep on track and keep the work focused. We can guarantee you we had fun along the way as John slipped gags and jokes into random paragraphs. The fun was also a result of achieving the purpose we had set out to achieve. In fact, the more we focused on the writing, the more fun we had.

When you know your purpose, you are drawn to accomplishment. For decades, motivational speakers have pointed out the need to have goals. They tell us it's impossible to hit a target that doesn't exist. So what is your purpose in life? Does God have something He wants you to accomplish during your lifetime? We can assure you He does!

The Bible tells us in Ephesians 1:4, "God chose us in Christ before the foundation of the world to be holy and blameless before him." And verse 12 concludes, "We who first hoped in Christ have been destined and appointed to live for the praise of His glory." Notice here how God had you and me in mind before He created the universe! As the Master Architect with His Great Blueprint, He pictured each one of us, He planned every single one of us, right down to the purpose He had for us! WOW! Think about that! God had you in mind before He created the universe. He prepared for every single one of us, a life of meaningful purpose!

Are you already living that life of meaningful purpose that God designed for you? Listen to Psalm 96, "Sing to the Lord, bless His name; tell of His salvation from day to day. Declare His glory among the nations, his marvelous works among all the peoples." Thousands of years ago, the psalm writers described for us who live by faith in the Lord, what a life of meaningful purpose is like! We are given the joy and the honor of declaring the glory of God to all the peoples of this earth!

Don't feel bad if you haven't understood this concept up until now. The disciples didn't get it at first when Jesus was on the earth. During His ministry, before the crucifixion, He said the same thing. He tried to get this across to His followers while He was with them, but like most everyone else, they did not understand at first! So, after Jesus was crucified and rose from the dead, He returned to His disciples and summarized His teaching to them. They finally grasped the big picture.

In fact, in all four Gospels, Jesus says the same thing! As we have mentioned previously, you're probably most familiar with the words in Matthew 28:19-20 (what is called the Great Commission), where Jesus said, "Go therefore and make disciples of all nations, baptizing them in the name of the Father and of the Son and of the Holy Spirit, teaching them to observe all that I have commanded you." You'll find the same sort of thing in the other three Gospels.

This is the life of meaningful purpose that God has created for us, that Jesus has redeemed us for, and for which the Holy Spirit has sanctified us! There is absolutely no doubt that God intends every single one of us who claim to follow Jesus Christ to live a life that declares the glory of God among all the peoples of the world! We are not designed, created, and redeemed just to live a life pursuing trivia!

All glory belongs to God! By glory, I mean splendor, value, and praise-worthiness. He deserves all our glory, not the other way around. We are designed to do HIS will! God has created us to put His name and His fame and His reputation on display! That happens when we share with others about His love and mercy and grace. It is clear in today's world that most people don't know much about love, mercy, and grace, and this is because they don't yet know Jesus!

Beginning the Journey

So how do we begin the journey of declaring the glory of God? There are two words that are critical to this life's purpose. Two words that keep popping up in scripture: "go" and "send!" To live that life of meaningful purpose as a follower of Jesus Christ, you want to be focused on being a goer or a sender! The only other option is to live in the trivial!

Imagine your life with a purpose, God's purpose! Imagine returning, as Darrel and one of the teams from *The Sending Place*™ recently did from Guatemala, where we were able to touch the lives of over 750 people, teaching them the Bible in a number of locations! We even helped serve lunch to the hundreds of people who live each day in the Guatemala City garbage dump. Believe us, that's something you will never forget!

Perhaps, you will be someone who is trained for a variety of tasks. You might teach English in the public classrooms of Russia, by using the Bible as their text, and watch the lives of young people change right before your eyes!

You may bring the glory of God to the villages of South Africa, preach and teach and pray, and help start new churches of believers! Some short-term missionaries do counseling; some lead Vacation Bible Schools, while some accomplish construction work. Teams to Brazil can use all those skills, while other teams perform medical work, teach in seminaries or other schools, or work with orphans and handicapped children, as we do in the Ukraine and India.

When you go, you go as servants of the missionary or mission agency in those other countries, and do the work of the Gospel that is most needed there. You can do this with the training we provide! Training is two Saturdays per month for five months. Some of the training is done using videos when you are too far from a training location for the Saturday sessions. Then, most mission trips last anywhere from ten days to three weeks.

If you are not preparing to go on a short-term mission team, then you can be a sender of those who are going! That means you are sending money on a regular basis to help train and send the goers when they ask you for the funds that are needed. You are excited when their support letters arrive. You are encouraging and praying for them constantly to keep satan away from distracting or harming them. The truth is, satan does not want any of them to go.

In other words, whether you are a goer or a sender you are living that life of meaningful purpose you were created to live, fully focusing on the main task of life— declaring the glory of God to all peoples.

You can commit yourself to being a goer, or to being a dedicated sender today. As a goer or sender, we invite you to partner with us at *The Sending Place*™. We see to it that you who are goers are well-trained, that all the details of travel, room, and board are arranged. Once you really get involved in world missions, you'll never be the same, for you will experience some awesome, exciting things! You'll have more joy, self confidence, self-satisfaction, fulfillment, and real adventure in your life.

"The Sending Place™" Vision

We hope you catch the vision as we have. Being involved in and/or supportive of *The Sending Place*™ is a great way to have a significant purpose in life. You have the opportunity to, with God, provide a facility where we will bring people in from all over the country, train them together right there, and then send them all over the world. We plan to send out hundreds of missionaries every year. Doing so requires the help of many committed senders who make it possible for the goers to go.

As of the writing of this book, we have already purchased property for that purpose near Redding, California. The next step is to raise a few million dollars to construct the buildings, and reach our full potential. If you want to see some of your money do great things in world missions, consider giving to *The Sending Place*™.

On the last night of His life, Jesus prayed to His heavenly Father and said this, "I glorified you on earth by finishing the work that you gave me to do." (John 17:4) In other words, Jesus had completed the life of meaningful purpose He came to live, and that gave glory to God.

It is our prayer that you are able to say that you have finished the work God gave you to do the day before you die. You really can if you live that life of meaningful purpose instead of a life of trivial pursuit!

Chapter 5

This Could Be You!

"Only by being there and feeling and smelling for themselves will they understand the need."

-- George Verwer

Questions To Enhance Your Reading

1. What is my place in the Great Commission?

2. How would I feel knowing I sent someone and made these stories possible?

3. How would my life be more fulfilled if I experienced God using me this way?

4. How can one person make a difference?

POSSIBLE MISSION TEAMS

What will you or the people you send actually experience when you go on a short-term mission? There are many answers to this question because there are many different opportunities to serve in God's mission field. *The Sending Place*™ trains and sends short-term mission teams to a wide variety of ministries around the world. The following are true stories from past missions which you could experience on a mission trip.

PETROZAVODSK, RUSSIA

Excitement and anticipation have kept you up most of the night. Everything you have trained for is about to be put into action! A new school day has begun here at Lyceum #1, a public school of Petrozavodsk, Russia, and ten students are looking at their new teacher with wondering eyes. You recognize that little flip-flop you feel in your stomach is caused by excitement and you can't wait to get started. You realize that the new teacher for these students—is YOU! This is what you have been training for through *The Sending Place*™. This is why you have studied and practiced your curriculum, and flown half way around the world. You are here to teach English to these students, but not the way you were taught in your country. You will have the privilege to use Bible stories in order to do that. Your faster rate of breathing and heart rate remind you that you really are eager to get started. How exciting to know these young minds are about to hear about Jesus, the Savior and Lord of all people. To them, it may start out as a way to learn better English, so they can be more successful in their world. But you know it's that and infinitely more!

Most of the students seem open to learning more about both English and Jesus. At lunch time, you enjoy seeing the other missionary teachers who are on your team, and you discover they are having experiences similar to yours. You are only half way through your day. In the afternoon, you work using the techniques you have learned from *The Sending Place*™, in order to keep the students' attention, and by the time the school day is over, you know you will probably sleep quite well tonight, unlike the night before, when you stayed awake pondering your new role as teacher.

Walking toward your host family's apartment, you see broken beer bottles everywhere, with dogs meandering around, and you're amazed at the number of young women who are pushing their babies in what you consider old-fashioned baby buggies. In a short while, you arrive at your apartment building, an eight story structure built around an open square.

Opening the door you enter the building, your eyes have trouble shifting to the darkness of the drab hallway, and with a musty smell in your nostrils, you head for the stairs, where that hike up to the fourth floor awaits you. Now you know why your training included the encouragement to "get in shape."

When you arrive at the apartment, you are amazed at the contrast, as it is very homey and comfortable inside, with the delicious aroma of dinner welcoming you. You enjoy visiting with your host family, and getting to know more about these hard-working people.

Your host for this ministry is "East European Missions Network," founded by Pastor Don Richman, and now headed up by Pastor Bill Moberly. Each year, they arrange for short-term missionaries to come to Russia, so that hundreds of children can learn better English, while they come to know how much Jesus loves them, and has a plan for their lives.

KISUMU, KENYA

Walking down the streets of Kisumu with other members of your short-term mission team, your heart begins to ache as you see hundreds of "street boys" sitting or wandering aimlessly. You wonder what that thing is that seems attached to their chest. As you get closer to one of the boys, you realize it is that bottle of glue you have been hearing about! Each boy finds a way to attach that open bottle of glue close to their face, so they can sniff it often, thus inebriating their minds from the pain and hopelessness of the moment. Their drab eyes are far away, perhaps in some happier place than they find themselves. But you know that look is actually caused by the poisonous effects of glue-sniffing. With every sniff the real price of their temporary euphoria is dead brain cells. Beginning with that first inhalation the wondrous brain God gave them begins to die.

Here in Kisumu, as in other places of Kenya, boys by the thousands are wandering the streets on their own, either orphaned by AIDS or some other tragedy. They may have been kicked out of their family's home at a young age, unwanted by their parents because in that culture daughters are of value to the family, as they bring in a dowry when they are married. These boys have no hope and no plans for the future. They are just trying to survive, searching for a scrap of food that will keep them from being too hungry tonight.

You try to talk with some of these boys, and they actually listen, though their glue-sniffing ways make them seem distant, and you wonder how much they understand of what you are saying. As you return with your team to "Agape Children's Ministry," you notice more than you had before how these 110 boys look so much different than the ones who were still on the street.

Having replaced glue-sniffing with a love for Jesus Christ, these boys are much more alive, with dancing eyes, and real hope for the future! Your hosts, Pastor Dan Schmelzer and his wife Patty, have much for you to do in this excellent ministry, which was started by Darla Calhoun in 1993. These boys are no longer homeless, as they live right here at Agape.

You think back when earlier in the day, it was your turn to teach the Vacation Bible School lesson to the twenty students in the seventh grade class. You told them the story of the lost sheep, and how the good shepherd loves each sheep so much, that he goes out and finds even one lost sheep, and carries it back on his strong shoulders. You have allowed God to use you as His good shepherd and send you thousands of miles to seek out and help his sheep. Just as you see yourself as a character in the story, so do the boys. They identify very well with such a reality of their own lives, and are glad to be loved by such a Lord who will search for them and not leave them alone.

That evening, you return to the nearby hotel, where you cannot get one particular boy out of your mind. You can't help wondering what his future will be. He is already so precious to you; you wish you could put him in your suitcase and take him with you! You realize how blessed your own family has been, and your heart is heavy thinking about the street boys. Yet, there is much hope for the boys who know the Lord at Agape, and you begin to understand the value of your mission trip. God has changed your perspective! The investment of your time and the training you went through clearly were worth it. The difficulties you experienced in your travels now seem insignificant. You have grown, stretched and are now able to imagine accomplishing great things for God when you return home.

JOHANNESBURG, SOUTH AFRICA

Some of these names sound familiar as you have heard them in the news over the years as South Africa transitioned away from apartheid. Driving down the main streets of Soweto, a suburb of Johannesburg, you see thousands of homeless Africans sitting or walking all around you. Yes you heard right, not one or two like you might see in a downtown area back home, but thousands of people of all ages are mingling, with very little to do, and very little hope that tomorrow will be different. Their eyes look sad, and often hopeless. Laughter is rare.

You turn onto the side streets, some of which are paved but most of which are yellowish dirt. You see rows of homes on each side of the street. These were built by the South African Government, to try to give homeless people a place to live. Hastily built out of concrete blocks set on a concrete slab, these tiny abodes have a toilet, a sink and two electrical outlets. That's it. As each home is finished, some government worker goes to the next name on the list of homeless people who have signed up, and gets word to them that they can now move in. Now the family must somehow find beds, table, chairs, etc., but at least they are out of the harsh sun and the beating rain. As you drive along, you notice that there are thousands of these homes, with more being built every day. And still the homeless come. As bad as conditions are in much of South Africa, they look great to someone living in neighboring Mozambique, or other African nations!

But you are not here to just look at small houses or homeless people. You are not a spectator or tourist. You are a short-term missionary, who is here to show the love and grace of Jesus to as many people as you can! Your hosts, Jay and Sarah Gerhart of Africa Ministry Resources, have been laying the groundwork for your mission trip.

Each day you visit the homes of these people, where the families are struggling with the misery of HIV, or are mourning the loss of a loved one due to AIDS, or both. In each home, you help pray for the family, and you are warmed by the peace and hope God brings them through you.

In the afternoon, you arrive where children are waiting for you to lead a Vacation Bible School, complete with Bible stories, crafts, and fun. In the middle of all this disease, homelessness, misery, and hopelessness, the children come eagerly, enamored with you. You are one of the strange people from America, and they are very open to hearing about this Jesus.

As you teach these children, you are amazed how they will sit and listen to you for hours! You are not used to this in America, where children are believed to have a short attention span, and often flit from one toy, game or video to another. Not so here in South Africa. You get these children's full attention, for as long as you want it!

After a week or so working in the Soweto area, your team heads out into the bush, driving about six hours to a remote village in northern South Africa. Here, you will do more of the same things, and you may even have the chance to help start a new congregation in a village targeted by Pastor Thomas Maphophe, who partners with Africa Ministry Resources, to encourage church planting strategies in that area. You know *The Sending Place*™ has helped start and minister to other congregations there.

Staying in the homes of the village, you live with these gentle people who will do everything possible to make your stay a pleasant one! Their hospitality is truly amazing, much better than you are used to back home, as they keep you well fed with chicken, rice, and pap (a type of corn meal). They, too, are eager to hear what you have to teach them or preach to them about Jesus the Christ, not only your Savior, but theirs as well!

As you return to Johannesburg, you take a little different route than you took coming up here, which takes you through Kruger National Park. As you drive through the park for a few hours, there is no doubt that you really are in Africa! Elephants, giraffes, zebras, and impalas are downright common, but you have to stay alert to see the occasional lion, hippo, kudu, leopard, and African buffalo.

Once you return home, you realize you have changed. There is an ache in your heart that just won't go away. Some of the people you grew to love may not be alive if you return there in a couple of years. Hearing that 25% of the South African people (ten million people) are forecast to die in the next ten years due to AIDS, you want to share that with your church friends and your congregation's Mission Board. You want to keep helping the on-going ministries in South Africa, which are trying to turn the tide from death to life. You realize you have become a world Christian, with a view that is much larger than the tiny world on which you used to be focused. Now, you multiply your effectiveness as you work to expand the view of others in your congregation.

GUATEMALA CITY, GUATEMALA

The dust swirls underfoot and all around you as you walk down into the canyon. The stench of garbage mixes with the dust, and you are surprised that it does not bother you as much as you thought it would, because you are too busy focusing on other things. You must stay alert to keep out of the way of the constant rush of garbage trucks going down into the canyon with heavy loads of garbage, and returning empty. Well, almost empty. You watch with nervous concern as young children and teenagers jump on the back end of the truck to have a little fun, before they jump off as the truck picks up speed.

You are surrounded by people combing through garbage. Three hundred, maybe four hundred people with Mayan ancestry, searching for things they consider of value to them. They are competing with hundreds of vultures who are gliding and hopping all around, fighting for their own treasures.

"One man's trash is another man's treasure" comes to mind as you stand in awe, out of the path of the trucks, and watch this human activity that you have never before considered for yourself! Yet another quote comes to mind, as you think of Genesis 1:27, "So God created man in his own image, in the image of God he created him; male and female he created them." What you are thinking and what you are seeing clash in your brain? Created in the image of God...scouring through garbage...Your mind races, but things just don't fit together. It has never been clearer to you that God's paradise was broken when we chose to sin.

This is not what God created but what humans have created.

Yet there's no time to continue your thoughts. The pickup has arrived from "The Servant's Heart" ministry, carrying lunch for about 150 people. Most of the residents will not take the time to come over for lunch, as they seem afraid they will miss out on some treasure if they do.

You go over to the pickup and help to pass out the soup, lemonade, and potato chips that have been brought that day for the people. They line up quietly and respectfully, waiting their turn for the simple lunch the ministry provides that day. As you pass out the food, you try to catch their eye, so you can make human to human contact with them, but almost no one will look at you. Their eyes are sad and hopeless, and tend to look down, not up. Their hands have a layer of black that does not look like it can be washed off any time soon. Bandages on those hands try to keep out the overload of germs from getting into the cuts and scrapes beneath.

You notice a young boy, maybe ten years old, cradling something in his arms. As he gets closer in the line, you recognize them as two hamburgers in McDonald's wrappers. Nearby, a large pile of garbage left by an earlier truck clearly shows it had come from a local McDonald's ™ restaurant. This young lad must have been one of the first to enter that little mountain of garbage. The day or two old sandwiches he holds are such treasures to him; he won't even eat them yet!

Your mind is racing, and your determination to help this ministry reach these people wells up inside you. This is why you trained for ministry through *The Sending Place*™. This is what you have flown thousands of miles to do. Later that afternoon, safely back at the ministry buildings right on the edge of the city dump, you look forward to leading Bible study with the 120 children who will show up, or the 70 adults who will come.

"The Servant's Heart," begun by Carla Burnell, is a ministry of love, working daily with hundreds of people who call the Guatemala City Garbage Dump their home.

Monday through Friday each week, food is prepared and taken down into the dump, to touch all who will come with the taste of God's love. In the process, they are invited to come to the ministry for Bible study, and some more of God's love.

When the people arrive at the ministry, they are clean and eager to listen. If you had not been down into the dump, or visited them in their homes, you would not have a clue where they spend most of their time. They are friendly but shy. You are glad you are there, trying to help change their lives, to a life filled with hope, and plans for the future. God has a plan for each one of them—they just have not quite learned it yet. But because of the faithful work of "The Servant's Heart" and the short-term mission teams they host, people's lives are changing, and you are glad to be a part of that!

When you return home, you know you will never be the same again. Things you used to take for granted, like clean hands for lunch, and a roof that covers your entire house, are recognized as quite a luxury. You understand better now that people in other cultures have incredible needs, while you have been given incredible resources to help meet those needs. The Bible's frequent teaching, that we are blessed to be a blessing, has now become very real to you. You want to help poor and destitute people more than before, and you work harder in your congregation to get them to do the same.

BILA TSERKVA, UKRAINE

Another exciting day dawns as you get up in the simple yet clean home, and eat the unique breakfast of open-faced sandwiches with cheese and meats your host family has prepared for you. Then after morning team devotions, it's off with the rest of your team to the Boys' House, where you help lead a Vacation Bible School for about 50 of the boys, while another 100 are not allowed to come out. The children range in age from 5 to 24, and have never known the love of a family. They have lived in this institution their whole lives.

Even though you speak different languages, you see what they are saying by the look in their eyes. They are craving your love and attention. Your heart fills with pain, and your eyes fill with tears as you realize they need so much affection. As the Vacation Bible School session begins, you begin to play games that promote interaction, so that you can touch as many boys as possible. They respond warmly to your touch and in fact, often linger for more.

Then it is your turn to teach the morning lesson. You look into the boys' eyes and you see a great hunger—a hunger to learn about this Jesus who loves them so dearly, and who cares for them and has a plan for them. You fight back the tears, to get your point across. You are glad you trained so hard, and practiced your lessons well before coming here.

Now it's time for two other members of your team to lead the craft session. You are amazed at the creativity and the talent of these boys, who love to be complimented and stroked in the process. The regular teachers are quite reserved, as they stand and watch what your team is doing.

At the day's closing of the Bible School, the boys sing the songs about Jesus, and they are thrilled to sing about His love. You would like to sing louder yourself, but the lump in your throat prevents it, as your heart breaks thinking about them living in an institution for the rest of their lives, never knowing the love of a family. That is one part of their culture you do not like.

You are glad to take a breather, have lunch with your team, and enjoy the staff of "God's Hidden Treasures," your host ministry. The director, Nita Hanson, is a very humble, dedicated servant of the Lord. It's good to be around her and her staff, as they help give you renewed energy for your afternoon.

After lunch, it's off to the Cerebral Palsy Center. Now your heart breaks in a different direction. These boys and girls do have loving families, as you watch their mothers and grandmothers attend this Vacation Bible School with them. But these children have severe disabilities, mostly physical, though some are affected mentally, as well.

Here, you do what you did in the morning session, but these children have great limitations, so you adjust the activities to each person. Each child is thrilled to receive such personal attention, and you are very glad you are there to give it to them. Your heart aches for the children and for their families amidst such huge disabilities, but you still share with them that God has a plan for their lives, even though they may be quite different from what they would like to be.

As you say good-bye to the children in both places at the end of the week, you are not crying alone, as many of the children break down in deep sobs as they hug you and say their good-byes. You are so glad you shared this special week in their lives. You discover that the thoughts you had at home that being away for so many weeks would be so long now seems so short. You wish you had even more time to stay and be involved in their precious lives. Even the teachers at the Boys' House are now giving hugs and kisses, having warmed up to you because they see your love for the boys, which is truly Christ's love through you.

During the second week of your mission trip, you shift gears and visit the other ministries of "God's Hidden Treasures." You help deliver wheelchairs to handicapped people, some stroke victims, and some suffering from diabetes. You also have a tremendous opportunity to help serve 300 handicapped people at a city-wide picnic hosted by the ministry! For some of these, this is the only day of the year they can leave their homes, because they cannot get down the stairs of their apartments, and even if their building has an elevator, it is too small for their wheel-chair.

As you return to your home in the United States, you know you have changed. You have left your own little world behind, and can see through the eyes of a different culture. The people of the Ukraine are a strong people who have undergone deep pain, suffering, and hardship. World War II is not just a memory—it still affects them, with so many of their loved ones having been killed. The nuclear accident at Chernobyl is not just a memory either—it still affects many with tumors and other health problems. You know it is not just enough to go back home and feel thankful for all your blessings. You want your church friends and your congregation to get involved in helping to bring more of God's love to a wonderful people who have such great needs.

VISAKHAPATNAM, INDIA

It's 8:50 am, a warm, humid winter morning along the coast of southern India, and 700 well-mannered children in blue uniforms are lining up under the trees of the large school playground to hear what you are going to share with them for today's morning devotions. Some children are orphans, some come from families and homes in the nearby village, some are Christian, and some are Hindu, but you cannot tell one from the other at the moment. Their eyes are bright and they are eager to learn. You share from your heart, glad that the children can understand English, as you tell them a valuable lesson about Jesus. They seem to appreciate your brief devotion, as they get ready for the day's classes.

At 9:30 am, classes begin in this school run by "Christ for India," a ministry started in 1981 by Dr. P.J. Titus and his wife, Mary. This ministry trains nationals at their Church of the Rock Seminary to be pastors and evangelists to start native churches, and they begin pointing the children toward Christ at a young age.

Your focus here is to help to teach the 700 children about Jesus in their Nava Jeevan (New Life) Public School. You go to a classroom and teach them a Bible story, then lead them in a related craft. Your lesson takes longer than the allotted time, so the other students are out of that class session, and 50 to 80 of them are hanging in the doors and windows, eager for their turn with you! You also know that a few other members of your team are over at the Church of the Rock Theological Seminary nearby helping to teach the 160 native men and women who are training to become pastors in India.

If you have medical skills, you could also help serve the poor villagers at Jyothi Hospital, to help alleviate some of the suffering of the poor and destitute of the area.

You know Christians are a small minority of people in this enormous land, but here on the grounds of "Christ for India" you cannot tell. You are glad you trained for this ministry, so you can help strengthen and encourage these courageous people to go forth with the Gospel of Jesus Christ to a vast nation of people, many of whom have not yet heard this story.

On Sunday, you worship at a church in a village not far away. The native people worship with more enthusiasm than you are used to back home. It is hard to get used to being treated like some sort of rock star, but that's how they see you. You are much larger than they are, and you stand out in the crowd. They treat you and your team with honor and respect. They do get used to you and your team members, and they pray with vigor. One of your team members gives the sermon that day, and all the worshippers listen intently, as they sit on the floor.

As you are being driven back to the "Christ for India" mission house where you are staying together with the other members of your team, you ponder some of these strange sights and customs you have seen today. You are way out of your comfort zone, especially in the complete chaos of traffic, with pedestrians, bicycles, motorcycles, rickshaws, cars, buses, cows, and sheep all mingled together, and yet it is comforting to realize that, even though you have a very different culture than these Indian people, the Lord is in both peoples, and His love and mercy shine brightly. It's also exciting to understand, that some of you from both cultures will be in the heavenly kingdom together, and you'll be glad to see each other there! God is an amazing Lord!

When you return home, you know you will never be the same again! Things you used to take for granted, like air-conditioning and orderly traffic flow are recognized as quite a luxury. You understand better now the Bible's frequent teaching that we are blessed to be a blessing. You want to help other people more than you used to, and you work harder in your congregation to get them to do the same.

CHENNAI, INDIA

Over 500 pairs of eyes are staring at you and the other members of your team. These children have been given a break from their normal classes at school in order to gather to listen to the concert you bring to them. They are glad to get out of class for awhile, and see these strange people from far away, and hear what you have to say in song and word.

Your heart races and your mind is on overload. This is the moment you have been training for through "The Sending Place"! This is the reason why you have been rehearsing all those songs. This is the real reason God gave you talent for singing with such a fine voice! As you sing praises to the God of the universe, the children sense your joy, and their eyes dance along with your music.

After singing several songs, your team pauses, and it is your turn to give your testimony of faith in the Lord Jesus, sharing from your heart. You were afraid you could not keep the attention of 500 children, and you are pleasantly surprised to discover they actually want to hear what you have to say!

When the concert is over, you quickly gather up your musical instruments and your sound equipment, and the team heads for another school nearby, where you repeat the process all over again. You are excited about the prospect of singing to the children in two different schools each day for two weeks. It's hard to imagine that your music and testimonies will touch around 8,000 Indian children with the Gospel of Jesus while you are here!

This is a ministry set up by "Hindustan Bible Institute (HBI)," now headed by Dr. Bobby Gupta and his wife, Linnet. Their ministry has already touched the lives of many thousands of native Indian people, and your team will add to that number.

You never dreamed this is where your talent would take you, but you know you will never be the same, especially after you also have the opportunity to visit some nearby villages that were destroyed by the Dec. 26, 2004 tsunami. The power of water is awesome, as the concrete walls of the homes were blown apart. The surviving villagers are warm and friendly to you, as you visit with them in their temporary tent homes further away from the ocean's shore. Their lives have been completely changed, and they are more open than they have ever been to hear about this Jesus who loves them and has a plan for them.

When you return home, you sing in your church choir with more urgency than ever before, and you try to recruit others to go with you on your next mission trip. You finally understand what life is about for a follower of Jesus—that you are here to proclaim Him as Lord to the peoples of the world. As a world Christian, with your mind now on the whole world, not just on your little corner of the town you live in, you want others to understand the urgency of the moment. It is frustrating at times, but you push forward, eager to share with others this great Lord who brings salvation to all who will accept Him.

Chapter 6

When Will You Go?

"The great news is that short-term missions open up the mission field to 'ordinary people'. I hope you can see yourself as part of that wave."

-- Darrel Deuel

Questions To Enhance Your Reading

1. What is my place in the Great Commission?

2. Is my congregation moving forward or backward in the Great Commission?

3. What if Christians just stay where they are, and go nowhere to proclaim Jesus as Lord?

4. Where have I gone lately to preach His word?

When Will You Go?

Have you been to any football games recently? If you're at a high school or college game, especially if your team is behind in the fourth quarter, the cheerleaders will sometimes begin a simple chant when the offense takes to the field. GO...GO...GO...GO...It means it's time for the offense to get going and score some points, or you are going to lose.

But what happens if the offense goes nowhere, does not move the ball? What if there are no yards gained, maybe they even get sacked and lose yards, and go backwards. That's a real bummer for the fans—what a disappointment! I mean, what football fan wants to watch their team go nowhere and lose?

Do you realize that the very same is true in the Christian faith? God has a team on this earth that He calls "the church." He has put this team together. He has given us a wonderful playbook with which to train. He's given us all the strength and power we need to do the task, and get it done. He is cheering us on.

But what happens if we, "the church", do not go anywhere? What if we just stay where we are right here in the United States, or even lose ground where we are? Then God is not pleased, because He does not want His team to go nowhere, and lose!

Are you on God's team? That is, are you a member of His church? Are you ready for action, trained to do the task He put you on this team to do? Do you study your playbook (the Bible) regularly, and benefit from what it says? Do you listen for God's direction as you read it? Are you willing to follow the plays he calls (obedience)? Many Christians just settle for a once a week encounter with the God of the universe and just show up for church. Instead of discovering the excitement of being in the game, they just sit on the sidelines, unprepared to enter the game.

Jesus Came For Victory

Do you know why God the Father sent His Son, Jesus the Christ, to earth to become a man 2,000 years ago? He sent Jesus to win victory! Thousands of years earlier, satan had tempted the first people God created, and they fell for it. They wanted to be like God, not just human, and when they disobeyed God, satan won. Everything on the earth, everything in the universe, lost. Ever since, things here have been a mess and people are cut off from God.

But God knew it was only a temporary loss. He immediately had a plan ready for winning the victory once and for all. That's what Jesus is about. He came to win. God the Father had an unusual way of winning victory. Victory over satan and evil and death would only come through obedience, sacrifice, suffering, death, and resurrection!

Jesus was obedient and faithful on Good Friday, willing to go to the cross to sacrifice Himself and suffer for the good of others. He won victory over satan and evil! On Easter, when Jesus rose from the dead and came back to life, He won victory over death, as well.

Wow, what a winner this Jesus is! He began forming His team while He was still on this earth. He called them disciples, which means followers! Jesus made it clear that He wanted His team, His followers, to be a winning team, too. As we should expect, they obeyed, sacrificed, suffered, and would go all the way He called them to go! His team would never win, if the members of that team chose to stay safe and comfortable in their cozy homes.

Jesus' Final Instructions to Us

We have to remember what Jesus said to His team after He rose from the dead. In all four Gospel accounts, Jesus said the same thing, as He summarized His teaching before He left the earth!

In Matthew 28, Jesus said, "Go therefore, and make disciples of all nations, baptizing them in the name of the Father and of the Son and of the Holy Spirit, teaching them to observe all that I have commanded you."

In Mark 16, Jesus also says, "Go into all the world and preach the Gospel to the whole creation."

In Luke 24, Luke summarizes Jesus' teaching when he says, "Repentance and forgiveness of sins should be preached in Jesus' name to all nations."

Finally, in John 20, Jesus says simply, "As the Father has sent me, even so I send you."

Where have you gone lately to preach His word? Unfortunately, most Christians these days in America have chosen to completely ignore this command of Jesus, and have instead wanted to stay safe and comfortable in their cozy homes, going nowhere for the Lord!

We, as Christians, have so much to give to this world of lost and hurting people! We have a fabulous playbook we call the Bible. Some of us even know it! But knowing the plays isn't enough. You need to get into the game and carry them out if you want to be obedient.

Darrel speaking: In my role as Director of *The Sending Place*™, in addition to preaching in a different church almost every Sunday, and visiting many others, I also talk with missionaries and leaders of other mission agencies from many different denominations. As Christians, we often take pride in our doctrine. We pride ourselves in how we worship, but we keep it to ourselves! The vast majority of Christians have gone nowhere to proclaim Jesus this year, and have no intention of going anywhere next year! That is not pleasing to God.

Recently, I was with my daughter Jamie, who is an amazing mission team leader herself, as she and I visited over a dozen churches in the Minneapolis area. One church had over 2,000 members and 4 worship services each weekend. The pastor proudly gave us his business card, which boldly quoted their mission statement as being Jesus' words from Matthew 28—that this church's mission was to go and make disciples of all people everywhere. Where had their members gone to do that? Nowhere yet! He was reluctant to partner with us right away, so we could help them move forward. They were thinking about "easing" into it. Easing into obeying Jesus' main command? What's with that?

I did not know whether to laugh or cry. Thousands of members had made the Great Commission their mission statement, but no one was going anywhere! How tragic! How long will so many Christians persist in ignoring Jesus' command to go?

The theme verse for *The Sending Place*™ is Luke 10:2, where Jesus says some very true but tragic words, "The harvest is plentiful, but the laborers are few: pray therefore the Lord of the harvest to send out laborers into his harvest."

We hope all of you already are, or will now start, praying regularly and mightily for the Lord to send out those laborers. But be careful. As you pray about that through faith and obedience, you just might realize that He wants to send you!

Indeed, the work of world mission is not something God wants a few people to do! Most National Church Offices are sending fewer and fewer missionaries, at a time when the world needs more and more.

Interesting...As we hear Jesus in Matthew, Mark, Luke and John say GO...GO...GO...GO, our team is often going backward, instead of forward!

It's Time for Us to Obey

Clearly, it's time for us to stop this apathy and lack of obedience! Perhaps the time has come for a new kind of missionary outreach. It is easy to think that the way we have been doing something for years and years is the only or best way. Sometimes we need to let go of the past and be open to new opportunities and techniques of ministry. Many churches have met the worship needs of their members by creating contemporary services. New music is heard and is meeting the needs of more church members.

Missions also need to change to continue to carry out God's command. It is time to recognize that the current trend in world missions seems to be moving away from thinking about a missionary as some very unique person who is willing to move to Tibet for 30 years, and recognize that God is raising up a multitude of faithful followers who are willing to go overseas and preach and teach his word for a few weeks or months at a time! *The Sending Place*™ is on the cutting edge of this new missionary focus.

The great news is that short term missions when carried out by individuals who are trained can be very effective. Not only that, but it opens up the mission field to "ordinary people." We hope you can see yourself as part of that wave!

Oh, there is still a need for long-term missionaries, and some are still going, thank God. But the reality is, most of us will not be doing that. Now more than ever almost all of us really can enter the world mission field and go overseas for two or three weeks at a time, and do great things.

The Value of Short-Term Missions

So what is the value of a short-term mission team? Well, let's look at someone who has been considered to be the greatest missionary of all time, the Apostle Paul. What type of worldwide missionary work did Paul do? He carried out his work primarily, as a short-term missionary!

He kept going on one short-term trip after another, but in most cities where he traveled, you would have to say he was a short-term missionary. By that we mean, the book of Acts shows he was in Corinth for about 18 months, he was in Philippi for just a few days, he went to Thessalonica for about 3 weeks, in Greece for 3 months, in Troas for 7 days, and so on, and so on. In some of those cities, a new church was born before he left town.

What about today? Because we train all of our teams very well, we at *The Sending Place*™ see great results overseas in just two or three weeks worth of work.

One of our teams to Russia went right into the public school classrooms, teaching English, but using the Bible as their textbook! We used Luke 15 as our text, so the students would learn about the lost coin, the lost sheep, and the lost son. Because of this, they learned that they were lost without Jesus, while at the same time learning English. Many students came to know Jesus and believe in Him, right there in the classroom.

One of our teams that went to Kenya worked with abandoned and orphaned boys at Agape Children's Ministry, and also visited boys who were still on the streets. They also taught them the message that they were lost without Jesus, and again, lives were changed.

Because of the training our teams received, these two ministries in Russia and Kenya are now recommending that any future teams of missionaries, wherever they come from, should train through *The Sending Place*™ before they arrive! We do appreciate their confidence in us.

One of our teams that went to South Africa was the first team that had gone to work with missionaries Jay and Sarah Gerhart, who are excellent hosts. One short-term mission team helped start two new churches while we were there. Up in the village of Phaweni, we raised funds to build a church building. But then, the village headmaster saw what that new church was doing, and asked them if they would add on enough space to have a school for the whole village, since there was absolutely nothing of any kind of service in that place!

So building plans were changed, more money was raised here, and in just a few months after our team left that village, a very large, new building was in use. We are sending more teams back there in the future, to start more new churches! You can be a part of that joy and excitement if you answer God's call and register to go! With our help and training, you will be able to make an impact in the mission field.

The key to successful short-term mission trips is training. Extensive training prepares the people so that they hit the ground running when they arrive. Possible obstacles are not a surprise because they have learned what they may be, and how God has overcome them in the past. Also, we train them in what to do when they return and as a result their local congregation can catch the vision of reaching the world for Jesus. It is important to remember that God called all of us to serve in the mission field. In addition to those who go, people we call goers, we also need senders. The senders become partners in world missions. They make it financially possible for the goers to go! The good news is that we can all make that happen. That's a key reason why *The Sending Place*™ exists.

You Can Do This

Believe us, there is no greater work, no more exciting way to spend your time on this earth, than going to preach the Gospel! If you are reading this book, you can do this. God is not an exclusionary God. He didn't command some of us to go. He didn't say to go and make disciples of the nations when it is convenient. He didn't say to wait until your life was perfect (in fact we know by his own admission that Paul's was not). He did say GO! We've seen missionaries up to 86 and 87 years old serving just fine! God's call is for you to be on His team, not just sitting on the bench, but on the field and in the game. To go and make disciples of all the nations, is something most all of you really can do, as long as you have the training to do it well!

Not everyone will say yes to this at any one time. The Bible, therefore, gives us the concept that at any given time, there are two kinds of people on this team that we call the Christian Church. As we mentioned before there are goers and there are senders. That's it. There is not a third option!

For those of you who say yes to becoming goers, you will learn so much and discover how much God really is in your life. Your relationship with God will grow stronger than you can now imagine. You will get trained and be ready to go...But goers will not be able to go, unless the rest of God's people do the sending!

Senders provide the money which allows the goers to go! Plane tickets to far away places are not cheap, especially when we find that our missionaries prefer that we buy round-trip tickets, not just one way! We like to feed and house our missionaries while they are doing God's work, too. So, money is necessary.

How can you get involved? If you feel called to be a sender, it is important to make it part of your everyday life. Our current senders have found it important to set aside money from every paycheck to support *The Sending Place*™ and those who go.

We have to be honest with you that many of our senders see so much happen as a result of their participation in world missions that they oftentimes become goers. After all, scripture tells us that where our money is, so is our heart. By investing in sending missionaries around the world in short-term missions, our hearts become committed and we find ourselves wanting to go.

Both "Goers" and "Senders", must be fully focused on taking part in this enormous task that lies in front of us—to go and make disciples of all the people in this world.

So, which are you? Has God led you to step out in faith and go, or do you feel called to use the resources God has provided you to send others? Remember, you are either one or the other if you're on the Lord's team!

If you find yourself to be a sender, we hope you are led to support *The Sending Place*™ as it trains and sends more and more short term missionaries into the world to win the victory, proclaiming Jesus as Lord, to the ends of the earth!

Chapter 7

Is Your Faith As Big As You Want It To Be?

"Everyone has faith. The question is; in what do you put your faith, and do you act on your faith?"

-- John W. Drebinger Jr.

Questions To Enhance Your Reading

1. What is my place in the Great Commission?

2. How strong is my faith?

3. What or who do I trust above all else?

4. When was the last time you did something for God outside of your comfort zone?

What If My Faith Isn't Big Enough For Me To Go?

We are sure you have met people whom you believed had incredibly strong faith as a Christian. If you only had the faith they had, you would be able to serve God in very dramatic ways. We began to wonder how can we measure faith, and do different people have different levels of faith. The more we thought about it the more we realized we all have and use faith every day. Hebrews 11:1 tells us, "Faith is the assurance of things hoped for, the conviction of things not seen."

If faith is believing in the unseen, then how often do we believe or trust in that which is unseen? Now, we're not talking about anything mystical at this point, rather those things we encounter every day. We would be willing to bet that you displayed a degree of faith even as recently as a few minutes ago. If you are sitting down you displayed faith when you sat down in your chair. How so? Simple. We would be willing to guess that before you sat down you didn't examine the chair for flaws or damage. You didn't question its design or check for its load limit. You just sat down and had faith it would hold you.

You have references in the past that allow you to have that level of faith in a chair. You probably have never had a chair break as you sat in it, so your faith in chairs strengthens every time you sit down and don't go crashing to the floor. If you ever have gotten into an elevator, you displayed faith in action. You had faith that someone had maintained the elevator and its parts so you could safely ascend to a high elevation without endangering your life. You didn't inspect the cables for wear. You probably didn't check to see when the last inspection was made. You just got in and up you went. Once again, your faith was strengthened.

We may want to create a better distinction for that last statement. You see we don't think it was your faith that was strengthened. It was your faith in elevators that was strengthened.

Do You Have The Faith of an Atheist?

Even atheists have and display faith. It's just that they choose not to place that faith in God. It may be impossible to live in today's world without faith. Every day you and I put our trust and faith in other people and things without any hesitation. We have to or we would be immobilized, checking and testing everything throughout the day. Think about it. We aren't immobilized in our daily activities but we have become immobilized spiritually because we fail to exercise our faith in God and His will for our life.

Where Do You Place Your Faith?

Our faith is something we all have; the key is where are we placing our faith? For many Christians, we fail to put our faith in God to the same degree we are willing to put our faith in an elevator or a chair. Because we never take opportunities to put our faith in God, our faith in Him is never strengthened. A powerful faith in God comes from building references in our mind that God is faithful. Intellectually or from a biblical viewpoint, we may agree that God is worthy of our faith, but as James pointed out, "Faith without works is dead." Perhaps that is the significant meaning of that verse. Faith that is not exercised by placing it in action for God never grows, and if you aren't growing you are dying.

Strengthening Your Faith

Now that you know you have sufficient faith to accomplish what needs to be done in life, you need to build your faith in God. How do you do this? By trusting every day more and more in God and what He promises. When it comes to missions, we have an incredible promise that should give us all the confidence we need to step out and take action. Jesus, in the Great Commission, said He would be with us until the close of the age. How can we do anything but trust our personal Savior that He will not leave us alone with this task He has asked us to accomplish?

Comfort Zones

To help you understand how to grow your faith, let's talk about how it works. First, each of us has what can be called a comfort zone. Imagine a circle. Every one of your life's activities you are comfortable accomplishing fits within that circle. If you are asked to do anything that falls into the range of challenge or difficulty inside the circle, you are comfortable taking it on. On the other hand, occasionally opportunities occur in your life to do something which is outside the comfort zone. It is beyond what you are comfortable doing. When you are faced with a choice, do you do the thing that is challenging you, or do you remain safe inside your comfort zone and choose not to do it?

If you stay inside your comfort zone, nothing changes and there is no growth. If, on the other hand, you do take on the challenge, something wonderful happens. Because you go outside your comfort zone, you stretch beyond your limits. When you accomplish the task or action your comfort zone changes, and expands to include the new accomplishment and any other things of similar difficulty. Even other things that used to be outside your comfort zone have now become possible.

Most people make this stretch by trusting in themselves. That is great for self improvement, but as Christians we have an even greater ability to stretch and increase our comfort zone. When God places a challenge in our path we have an opportunity to put our faith and trust in God into action. The good news is that God wouldn't have offered it for us to do if He didn't know we would be able to accomplish it either with the skills and abilities we have or those He will provide.

We aren't trusting in ourselves - we are trusting in the Almighty God who created each and every one of us. So for us as Christians, whenever we take on a new challenge outside our comfort zone, we have a unique opportunity. We can take on the task and stretch our comfort zone, but we do it with the assurance that God is there to help us or knows we can do it. This takes it to a new level. We are stepping out in faith and trusting God. Every time you trust God you strengthen your faith. Every time you respond to His calling to serve Him, you strengthen your faith in Him. This is something you can do every day by trusting God with every aspect of your life.

Both Sending and Going Stretch Your Faith

So what does this have to do with going or sending? Simply, for many people committing a significant amount of money to support missions on a regular basis is a real stretch. By the way, tithing is a big way to stretch your faith. We want to make it clear we don't want you to take money you are currently supporting your local congregation with and merely transfer it to mission work. What will stretch your comfort zone and grow your faith is to increase your giving. If you don't tithe now, you can move in that direction by committing to be a "sender" who gives regularly to support *The Sending Place*™ and people who are "goers". If you currently tithe, you can trust God to allow you the opportunity to give more and see the results.

John has discovered the power of this approach over the past several years. In fact, he carries a scriptural quote in his wallet where he keeps his money. It is Malachi 3:10-12. "Bring in the whole tithe into the storehouse, that there may be food in my house. Test me in this," says the Lord Almighty, "and see if I will not throw open the floodgates of heaven and pour out so much blessing that you will not have room enough for it. I will prevent pests from devouring your crops, and the vines in your fields will not cast their fruit," says the LORD Almighty. "Then all the nations will call you blessed, for yours will be a delightful land," says the Lord Almighty. God has told us that tithing and giving extra clearly helps us.

It seems that once again God instructs us to do something for our benefit as much if not more than His. After all what does God need with our money? He created the universe. If He wanted the church to have more money all He would need to do is drop it in our laps. The fact is we benefit more by giving than God does.

For those who are called to be "goers", the opportunity for growth is awesome. No matter what your background or experience, each mission trip offers many situations which will cause you to stretch your faith and go outside your comfort zone. Even experienced "goers" find this to be the case. Each mission trip is unique and it has been our experience that each person faces their own unique challenges along the way. These challenges result in a rapid growth of their faith.

So if you want to grow faster than you ever have and be able to accomplish greater and greater things, whether at home or away, take the opportunity to respond to God's call and become a "goer" or a "sender" or both!

Chapter 8

Training Makes All The Difference

"If we don't adopt a commitment to excellence in our missionary thrust, I believe that we are going to be laying up big problems for ourselves in the future."
                                                    --George Verwer

Questions To Enhance Your Reading

1. What is my place in the Great Commission?

2. Is it really necessary to train missionaries before they go overseas? Aren't faith and a desire to serve enough?

3. What kind of things do I need to learn to be an effective short-term missionary?

4. Am I ready to learn how to be a more effective witness for God?

"What I want to tell you is that the team, you, The Sending Place™, sent here was the best team we have ever had—bar none! They came to do a job and went about doing it without any fuss, confusion, or problems. And how wonderfully they represented the Lord."
--Nita Hanson

TRAINING MAKES ALL THE DIFFERENCE

Can you just rely on God and go on a mission without any training? Sure, God is all-sufficient, but God has taught experienced missionaries through their experiences how to be most effective. It is definitely possible to learn from trial and error, but wisdom is learning from other people's experience. The Bible itself is a type of training for Christians. After all, why not just let us discover how to lead an abundant life? Proverbs is a book full of wisdom about how to live a great life and avoid pitfalls. If you have the wisdom to follow God's teachings, your life will be smoother and more effective. Well, when it comes to missionary work the same holds true. Over the years, thousands have responded to God's call to spread the Gospel and they have learned many things. Training allows us to accelerate your learning curve and your effectiveness. What if you could be as effective on your first mission trip as someone who went on five mission trips before they learned to be that resourceful?

Almost any job requires some level of training. Even an entry level position in a fast-food restaurant involves training. In fact, the success of many franchises is due to the lessons learned by the company and the training they provide. The training increases the likelihood of success. You certainly don't want a doctor to just do his or her best and see how it works out. You certainly want God to guide your doctor, but you want the doctor educated and trained before you enter the operating room.

We are Ambassadors

Picture a follower of Jesus Christ. The Bible says that Jesus' followers are ambassadors to the world. We do not represent a mere country though; we represent the God of the universe, creator of all things! Is it possible to be an excellent ambassador for the Lord without any study or training? No way! As with any human endeavor, excellence requires study, training, and just plain hard work.

It is no different being a missionary for Christ. We want to represent the Lord well; we want to know His will so we can obey His will. We need to train for the tasks that will be expected of us while we are overseas. It's important to understand what the Bible teaches, so our Bible story lessons we teach and sermons we preach are accurate and inspirational. All of that takes practice and training.

In addition, over the years, missionaries for Christ have encountered the obstacles that satan puts in their paths. Training allows us to share the challenges with you so you know ahead of time what to expect and how to handle it successfully.

At *The Sending Place*™, we are strongly committed to training all the missionaries we send! We train them to be teams, not just individuals going out to do a task. Jesus himself taught us that. He sent His disciples out two by two, as teams, to proclaim His word and do His work. A team that is unified, working together, is stronger than the sum of its parts.

It's All About Change

Training is all about change. While the missionaries train, they are changing, growing, and improving. When they are well-trained to do the task of a mission team, the people they serve overseas also change, because they experience God's love and grace in a powerful way. As the people come to faith in Christ, or strengthen their faith, their lives change, as they, too, grow and improve. When the missionaries return home and report the details of their mission trip to their congregations, the congregations will change too, as they become more committed to doing missions.

Training makes all the difference. An untrained team can actually have a detrimental impact on the people for which they do their mission work. We have talked with numerous host missionaries who have had negative experiences with untrained mission teams. We heard of one missionary, unprepared for the culture shock of the country in which they found themself, who stayed in their room for days. We know of other untrained mission teams who unintentionally offended their hosts and the host mission staff. Such things do not result in a successful mission trip! In fact, the more well-meaning someone is and the greater enthusiasm they bring to the project, the greater the possibility of causing a problem. One thing you will discover when you go on a mission is that there are many ways to accomplish a task around this world. We may mix cement in a cement mixer but in Africa they mix it in a hole in the ground. Which is better? It doesn't matter! What matters is our real purpose, which is to spread the Gospel, not teach better ways to construct, cook, or clean. Training allows our missionaries to stay focused and to make a difference in the spiritual lives of the people with whom we are working.

From Kisumu, Kenya

Pastor Dan and his wife, Patty Schmelzer, Administrators of Agape Children's Ministry in Kisumu, Kenya wrote:

"The experience we had this past summer, with the team from *The Sending Place*™ was outstanding. Much of the success is attributable to the fine preparation they received through *The Sending Place*™. Patty and I wish to commend *The Sending Place*™ for the wonderful spiritual and cultural preparation the short-term team received before they visited Agape Children's Ministry.

We love the balanced and mature leadership of the team leader, Jamie Deuel. She knew when to allow her team members to experience culture and when to warn them about offending someone or placing themselves or others in danger.

The team understood the need for flexibility, engaging the spiritual enemy through prayer and the Word, consulting with the administration in the country, as well as listening and responding to advice given to them on the ground.

Our complete confidence in *The Sending Place*™ allows us to recommend that all future teams who visit Agape Children's Ministry go through the training of *The Sending Place*™. May God richly bless this mission agency. For those who are considering the time for team preparation before taking a short-term foreign mission field trip, Patty and I highly recommend *The Sending Place*™. The few dollars that are spent by the team for training not only can alleviate problems for the team, but can also increase effectiveness of the team, increase safety, and bring joy to those in the country who are hosting the team. "Go and make disciples."

From Bila Tserkva, Ukraine

The Sending Place™ is committed to sending only well-trained teams into the field. Listen to what one host missionary had to say.

Dear Darrel,

I wanted to write and let you know how terrific the team was that you sent! We here at God's Hidden Treasures have received a lot of teams over the years since I came here and, to be honest, most of them take a lot of my time and are very draining. We do it because that is part of being a missionary—to allow others to have the opportunity to experience what God is doing in different parts of the world and to allow them an opportunity for God to work changes in their lives.

What I want to tell you is that the team you, *The Sending Place*™, sent here was the best team we have ever had—bar none! They came to do a job and went about doing it without any fuss, confusion, or problems. And how wonderfully they represented the Lord. I have never had a team commented on so much—the most typical being, "what a wonderful team this is" or "how nice ALL of the team is" and so on and so on.

I must tell you that this is the first team ever that I have been able to just enjoy, knowing that their leadership was in place, and that everyone came to do what God sent them here for. They were a real pleasure for me and I hated to see them go. Everyone whose lives they touched were enriched by them.

So, thank you so very much. And I hope to see another team come next year.

Blessings,

Nita Hanson

Director—God's Hidden Treasures

Bila Tserkva, Ukraine

Training really does make all the difference!

Chapter 9

Early Beginnings

"As we began to gear up toward sending our own teams on short-term mission trips, we wanted to be sure they had the proper training to make the mission a success for them and those they went to serve."

-- Darrel Deuel

Questions To Enhance Your Reading

1. What is my place in the Great Commission?

2. What is God doing to send more missionaries into His harvest?

3. What is my history of proclaiming Jesus as Lord?

4. What can God do through me?

How It All Started

Our story begins with and is best told from the perspective of Darrel. In Elk Grove, California, a suburban town just south of Sacramento, I was Senior Pastor of St. Peter's Lutheran Church. For 23 ½ years, I led a ministry that grew from 400 to 1,500 members. The congregation outgrew the small facility in the middle of town and bought ten acres a little north of town. At the time of purchase it was out in the country waiting for the rapid housing growth of the Sacramento area to surround it. Building the new facility began in the mid 1980's. Through four major construction projects, and the accompanying capital campaigns, the time, energy, and resources of the congregation were spent primarily on construction.

As a congregation, we continued giving benevolence money to many different ministries, both foreign and local, but we were not personally involved with the work of world missions. As we finally completed construction in 1995, we were feeling uneasy about that lack of personal involvement in proclaiming the Gospel overseas.

I began preaching on the subject, and taught an adult education course using the book "Let the Nations Be Glad" by Pastor John Piper. A powerful missions book, the course began to change the lives of people, to finally understand that we were designed by God to live a life of meaningful purpose, by declaring the glory of God to all the peoples of the world.

In talking with a variety of overseas missionaries, I discovered that they would rather have people stay at home unless they were trained. An untrained, short-term missionary created more problems than solutions, and in some cases set some missions back a step. As we began to gear up toward sending our own teams on short-term mission trips overseas, we wanted to be sure they had the proper training to make the mission a success for them and those they went to serve. We looked for where they could go for training.

Looking for a Training Center

We knew of other denominations that had active missionary training centers, and assumed the Lutheran Church did, too, though we had never heard of one. But there were none to be found, no matter what branch of the Lutheran Church we contacted! We were both surprised and disappointed.

We decided to seek out a non-denominational mission agency with which we could work. After considerable research, we chose the one that looked the best, and flew the director out to meet with our congregational leaders. As it turned out, they rejected us, because of denominational doctrinal issues. It seemed ironic that a non-denominational training center would be hung up on denominational doctrines.

So after much research, we were no closer to finding a missionary training center than when we began! During that process, our family was on a summer camping trip in southern Oregon. Our oldest son, Dan, had recently returned from a short-term trip to India, having gone with another Lutheran group from a congregation in Minnesota, where he received very little training.

I was looking at the local real estate guide, which was a common practice for me to do on our annual camping trip to southern Oregon. I was always looking for ranches of 200-300 acres that we might live on someday. I began to ponder a place of that size, and suddenly was struck with the thought of setting aside about 50 acres of the future ranch to build that much-needed Lutheran Missionary Training Center!

I shared that vision with my family, and everyone was excited about that prospect! It generated much discussion, in between fishing for trout and soaking in the gorgeous view of the surrounding mountains. God used what, at the time, seemed to be a negative event, the rejection by one training facility, to move us from the hypothetical dream to reality. The training center our family had talked about doing "someday," began to move on a fast track!

The Official Beginning

In the fall of 2001, my wife and I incorporated "Lutherans at Mission Body and Soul (LAMBS), Inc.", to be an independent Lutheran corporation. We adopted Luke 10:2-3 as our theme verse, "The harvest is plentiful but the laborers are few. Pray therefore the Lord of the harvest to send out laborers into the harvest. Behold, I send you out as LAMBS in the midst of wolves." We referred to ourselves as *The Sending Place*™ and that is the name that caught on.

About the same time, we formed a Board of Directors of like-minded people. The board decided we should begin immediately to train and send missionaries, rather than wait until "someday", after we had built the training center we envisioned. I was still a full-time Senior Pastor, and worked as Director of *The Sending Place*™ part-time. In January, 2002, we began training our first team; a group of five faithful women who would go serve in Petrozavodsk, Russia, hooking up with the ministry of "East European Missions Network."

Training went well, and our daughter, Jamie, led the team to Russia. The team did an outstanding job, touching the lives of 150 youth. Significantly, we were commended by the host ministry. The training had made a difference. Rather than being a burden on the host ministry, the team was a real asset and we were welcome to return. Jamie's previous mission team experience, having served in

Australia and India with other groups, helped guide the success. She has been given a tremendous heart for missions, and would love to lead mission teams year-round. Her smile tells the story of how much she loves to train and lead people to discover the joy of answering God's call.

Where Will the Training Center be Built?

Throughout 2001, I had been traveling whenever I could, searching for just "the right" piece of property on which to build *The Sending Place*™. The search took on a new urgency because the Board of Directors had decided we should step out in faith and purchase the property first, instead of waiting until everything was ready to go. This approach turned out to be a great model for those who would personally consider serving on a short-term mission in the future. It is easy to delay fulfilling God's call if you wait until everything is perfect. The Board realized that potential supporters would take the project more seriously if we already had the property. I traveled throughout the west, from California to Colorado, and all points in between. I had a certain criteria for which I was looking. It was important that it be a place missionaries in training would be exposed to the beauty of God's creation in the out of doors. Here, they could ponder their task, pray, and learn in peace and quiet, as in a retreat-type setting. Yet, it had to be fairly close to a large airport and affordable. Actually, since we had no money in the bank, "affordable" was an interesting concept! Once again a great model for the future missionaries of *The Sending Place*™. Instead of waiting until they could afford to go, many have trusted God, answered His call, and allowed Him to provide.

As hard as I searched, I just could not find the perfect place. By mid December, I was a bit discouraged, and decided to go on a goose hunting trip to northeast California, to relax a bit and get refreshed. As I sailed down Highway 299 a little east of the town of Redding, I happened to see a big sign on the left side of the road:

"FOR SALE, 350 ACRES." As I glanced at the gorgeous land behind the sign, I was fortunate I did not drive off the road!

350 acres. Less than fifteen miles from the Redding airport. Tremendous views of the surrounding mountains, including 10,000 foot Mt. Lassen. A creek running through rolling, oak-covered hills. Less than a mile from a pizzeria. As I checked off item after item in my mind, I became very excited. I had a hard time focusing on the successful goose hunt I had that weekend.

One thing kept bothering me, however, and that was the price. Such a gorgeous piece of land that close to town should be very expensive, undoubtedly way out of our price range, though to many people, it looked like any land would be out of our price range. Fortunately there is nothing out of God's price range.

Monday morning finally rolled around, and I called the listed realtor. $750,000 was the asking price. As high as that was, it seemed quite low to me, and I became even more excited. By the time I called the realtor back a few days later, 50 acres on the south side of the highway had already been sold, leaving 300 acres on the north side of the road for $650,000. Afraid of losing the rest of it, I contacted all the members of the Board of Directors, and they said, "Go for it." Several of them also said, "If we can get it for less than $600,000, we'll take it as a sign God wants us to have it."

I went for what I thought was quite a low offer, but might actually be possible, with plenty of miracles from the Lord. I submitted an offer of a $5,000 deposit, holding the property until late July, at which time we would make the remainder of a down payment of $150,000, with a total price of $550,000. Shortly, I received a counter-offer, changing the asking price to $600,000, but leaving the rest of the details as offered. Keeping in mind what some of the members of our Board of Directors had said, I did not accept. I counter-offered a total price of $575,000. In a few days, the answer was yes to all details!

Where Will the Money Come From?

This was one of those times when emotions run wild. I was excited, scared, and overwhelmed all at the same time. Things were falling into place more than I could have expected. But still, with the payment of the $5,000 deposit, we had to come up with an additional $145,000 in the next six months. Whenever I began to feel scared about that, I just kept remembering the words of Philippians 4:13, "I can do all things in Him who strengthens me." Matthew 19:26 promises, "With God, all things are possible." We strongly believed that God had given us the vision to do this project, and He would take care of it.

I had already begun to ask friends within the congregation as well as elsewhere within the Lutheran community to make pledges toward the future project, and I had a number of $10,000 and $5,000 pledges, but not nearly enough to make the down payment. We began to get the word out, and I asked those who had already pledged if they wanted to give their gift now or later. All of them gave their donation to help buy the property.

As the July 24 deadline approached, we were still a little short. On the day I had to mail the down payment, I needed to borrow about $3,000 to reach the full $145,000 amount. But at that point, the sellers began to disagree among themselves, and the close of escrow was delayed. By the time they reached agreement the following week, another $3,800 had come in! God had given us the exact amount when we needed it! He knew we didn't really need it when we thought we did.

Many people had been praying for the right amount of money to come in, and all rejoiced at the news that God had said yes! Escrow closed in early August, and on September 14, 2002, nearly 50 people traveled to the property for a celebration of worship and dedication. All were inspired as we set aside this place for the future training and sending of missionaries who would go with the Gospel, and declare His glory to all the nations. The plan is to keep about 100 acres for the project.

The Ministry Expands

As time moved forward, the ministry continued to expand. In January, 2003, eleven people began training to go on mission teams to Russia, Kenya and South Africa. Not all of the trainees were from St. Peter's Lutheran Church, so the call for God's people to go on mission trips through *The Sending Place*™ was beginning to grow beyond Elk Grove. We trained two Saturdays per month for five months.

The three well-trained teams went forth in the summer of 2003 and did excellent work. The team to Petrozavodsk, Russia, working with East European Missions Network, touched the lives of 200 children by teaching them English in the public school classrooms at a "Language Camp," using the Bible as the textbook. The teachers were thrilled to see some of the children's lives change right before their eyes.

The team to Kisumu, Kenya worked with over 100 abandoned and orphaned boys who had been brought in off the streets by "Agape Children's Ministry," and they visited with more boys who were still on the streets. The boys who were living at the ministry were eager to learn the Gospel, and live with hope for the first time in their lives!

The team to South Africa, working through "Africa Ministry Resources", helped start two new churches while there, one in Soweto, and the other in the northern village of Phaweni, touching the lives of 350 people while on their mission trip. After returning home, *The Sending Place*™ raised over $5,000 for the new congregation in Phaweni, and a beautiful concrete block facility has been built. It not only serves as the only church in the village, it was also built large enough to serve during the week as a school for all the children in the village!

In the fall of 2003, we trained a team of three eager people who went to "The Servant's Heart" ministry in Guatemala City, Guatemala. The team led Bible studies there and in other towns, touching the lives of over 750 people during their mission trip.

In the winter and spring of 2004, *The Sending Place*™ trained 46 people from nine different states and five different Lutheran bodies to learn together, unite together, and work together in Russia, the Ukraine, and South Africa! Teams going to Brazil, India, and Guatemala began training in the fall of 2004. The growth was remarkable, additional evidence that God was involved and He would receive the glory. We trained 5 people in 2002, 14 in 2003, and over 75 in 2004, with more and more people committing to go on short-term mission trips in the future!

As of the writing of this book, the work continues. Teams going on summer, short-term mission trips train from January through May, while teams going on winter short-term trips train from August through December. Training sessions are taking place in such far-ranging locations as the Sacramento and San Diego areas of California, the Phoenix, Arizona area, and the Minneapolis, Minnesota area. Dozens of congregations and hundreds of individuals and families are supporting the work of *The Sending Place*™ and partnering with us to proclaim Jesus as Lord to the ends of the earth.

I, John Drebinger, came to St. Peter's in 2002 because my family and I were drawn to be a part of a congregation that was so outwardly focused. I recognized that these people and the pastor who lead them had a heart for God. In December of 2003, Darrel asked me to join the board of directors of *The Sending Place*™. At my first meeting in January of 2004, I realized that Darrel and *The Sending Place*™ needed a book to tell the story of what God was doing in this wonderful organization. Several years earlier, I learned as a member of the National Speaker's Association the value of a book in spreading the word and helping people to take action. By March of 2005, the book was ready for publication and is in your hands today.

In an earlier chapter, we wrote that you might discover that you start out by becoming a "sender" and then as you discover the joy of world missions you want to become a "goer." This is what happened with John as he is going on his first mission trip as this book goes to press.

It's Only Just Begun

It is exciting that the history of *The Sending Place*™ has just begun. John discovered *The Sending Place*™ had a place for him. It also has a place for you! You can be obedient to God's call to all Christians to be focused on proclaiming the glory of God to all the peoples of the world by becoming a part of this exciting ministry, a ministry that is on the cutting edge of world missionary training. The fact that *The Sending Place*™ focuses on training short-term missionaries creates a whole new avenue for the "average" Christian to answer God's call. You can start training as soon as you choose the date to go overseas and have a life-changing experience, while you help change the lives of others. If you feel called to be a "Sender," you can send money on a regular basis to help pay the expenses of those who train and those who are going to spread the Gospel. Already, supporters are naming *The Sending Place*™ in their wills, donating real estate, as well as making special gifts and monthly donations! This rapidly expanding and effective ministry can do even more with your support. We would love to count you as being a partner with us in this greatest work of all!

Chapter 10

Reasons Why You Think You Can't Go

"We measure the worth of a hidden treasure by what we will gladly sell to buy it. If we will sell all, then we measure the worth as supreme. If we will not, what we have is treasured more."

--John Piper

Questions To Enhance Your Reading

1. What is my place in the Great Commission?

2. What are my "reasons" why I have not been active in world missions?

3. Am I willing to take risks to do God's will, or am I willing to live with the illusion I am safe and comfortable at home?

4. Have I been using any excuses to keep me from obeying God's will for my life?

Reasons You Can't Go and How God Can Overcome Them

For years, I John Drebinger, have worked with youth in the Boy Scouts of America, and one thing I have discovered is that when someone gives you an excuse it is rarely the real reason they don't want to help. Excuses are oftentimes expressions of what they know will be socially acceptable to the person they are turning down. For instance, people will seldom tell you they don't want to go on a mission because they are afraid. Rather than admit to succumbing to fear, they come up with a more acceptable and rational reason. This poses an interesting opportunity when persuading people to do something. If you try to solve the excuse they told you, they'll just give you another excuse. This can go on and on with excuses, frustrating any listener.

Why share this with you? There are two types of excuses. First, there are those that are just a façade or cover for the real reason you choose not to do something. Second, there are temporary obstacles we need to overcome in order for our life to continue on the path God intended. We recommend you look deep inside and listen to the voice bringing up any objection to your serving on a short-term mission team.

Is your excuse an obstacle that is temporary and just needs a solution, or is it an excuse masking the real reason? It is critical to remember there is no obstacle God can't overcome. The good news is when you face the real obstacle and allow God to help you break through it, your faith is strengthened along with your relationship with God. Instead of allowing satan to trick you into an excuse, use any obstacle as an opportunity to trust God and overcome it. In this chapter, after each excuse, we share how to overcome it, if it truly is an obstacle for you. If it is just an excuse you can skip the solution paragraphs as they don't matter.

As Executive Director of *The Sending Place*™, Darrel, travels extensively, preaching in congregations, speaking at conventions, visiting pastors and church leaders, encouraging Christians around the nation to "get out of the pews and onto the planes." Darrel invites them to get personally involved in the Lord's call to "Go and make disciples of all nations."

It is very sad that most church members, clergy and lay alike, have come to the conclusion that being a missionary is the job of "someone else." Just send a few dollars a year to the national church body you are a member of, and "they" will take care of world missions for you. Some name-less, unknown person from some other state will be trained and sent by the national church body. Since your congregation sent a few dollars to the national office, your responsibility for world missions is over.

Even though the Bible admonishes ALL of Jesus' followers to GO and declare the glory of God to the nations, even though the Bible tells us we are the light of the world, even though the Bible makes it clear we in the church of Jesus Christ are given the task to tell everyone what Jesus has done, most church members completely ignore these scriptures. They just live out their lives according to their own plans, their own desires, and their own agenda.

When we approach someone to personally get involved in world missions, oh, the excuses we hear! In fact, an entire book could be written on the "101 Excuses of Why I Cannot do Missions." Let us mention just a few in this chapter.

Excuse Number One:
"I DON'T HAVE TIME"

This is a common excuse usually stated as, "I'd love to go on a short-term mission but with my schedule I don't have the time." Time is very precious. In fact, it is more valuable than gold. Yet God expects us to give our treasures to serve Him. This is not only tithing money but giving time as well. Once again, scripture tells us in Matthew 6:21, "Where your treasure is, there will your heart be also." We invest our time in what we value in life. You can't tell me your family is very important to you if you spend all your time away from them. Too often we realize too late we have invested our time poorly. It has often been said no one on their death bed says, "I wish I had spent more time at the office".

Now we know many of you reading this book put in many hours of service to God in your local church and community. That is wonderful, but God wants us to experience ministry outside our own surroundings. He wants us to experience the joy and satisfaction of sharing the Gospel with the world. Once again by doing it His way we will actually improve our ministry at home. He strengthens us and shows us what is truly possible when He is obeyed.

For those of you who believe time is a major obstacle rather than an excuse we have a suggestion for you. Sit down with your calendar and select a date within the next eighteen months you would be able to serve on a short term mission. Select two weeks to start with if that serves your breaking through this obstacle. Then call us and we can let you know what mission trips are on the schedule or get you in touch with one that fits your calendar. We can't over express the importance of writing this specific date on the calendar. As a professional speaker, John Drebinger's schedule is booked months in advance yet he has always blocked out time for family, time for church, time for Boy

Scout events with his son, and special events with his wife, daughter, and son. Once the dates are on the calendar, it is easier to make them happen and much more difficult to cancel them. This is especially true when it comes to canceling something. You have to consciously decide what is more important, that which you are canceling or what is replacing it. It is then that you know which you value most.

How we spend our time tells a story about us and our priorities. Some people work eight hours a day, while others work eleven or twelve, and still others work none. Some talk to their spouse twenty minutes a day, while others do so only five minutes per week. Some make time to golf, watch sports on TV, go shopping, or surf the internet. Some take time to go to Bible Study every week, while others do not. Some set aside time to worship every week, while some do not.

Thus, we tend to take time to do the things that are important to us. If something is not important to us, we drop it way down on our list of priorities, so we just never manage to get around to it. That is, we don't have the time.

We hope you are one of those who takes the time to get personally involved in world missions, who personally makes the time to train for a mission trip and then climbs aboard that flying machine to cross the ocean in order to "Declare the glory of God to all the peoples"-- that you are someone who has and will make obedience to God a value or belief rather than a changeable priority in your life. You do not have any more time than anyone else, but God is important to you and it shows in how you invest your dollars and your time. After all, time is your life, and you can't say you have given your life to God if you hold back your time.

Excuse Number Two:
"I MET A MISSIONARY ONCE"

This is one of our favorite excuses. The person who uses this excuse will go into detail, where this missionary was serving, how they came to speak to the congregation once, maybe even what year it was. Since they met them in the flesh, because they have seen or known an actual missionary, their responsibility in world missions is over. The way this one works is that by identifying themselves as having a relationship with someone that is doing missions, they consider themselves involved.

If you have fallen prey to this excuse or believe your involvement already exists, ask yourself some of the following questions. When was the last time I prayed specifically for this missionary? How have I served them as a sender by supporting their work financially? If someone were to ask that missionary for a list of those who support their work and make it possible, would your name be on it? The answers to these questions bring to light our true involvement.

Excuse Number Three:
"MY CHURCH SUPPORTS (THE NATIONAL CHURCH BODY)"

Can you see a pattern here? Many of the excuses try to give the impression the person giving the excuse is, in fact, already involved in missions. This is a great approach if you want to avoid serving God in the mission field. After all, if you are already involved in the call that you are hearing in a sermon, this book or another source must be speaking to all those people who aren't involved yet. This approach is like being vaccinated against a disease. You get just enough to protect you from getting the real thing.

This is a common excuse, used by individual church members and whole congregations alike. They change God's command telling all of us to go. They have made themselves comfortable by misinterpreting the Bible to say it only applies to a few people in the church, certainly not to every follower of Jesus. Since it is not their responsibility, they are off the hook.

What is the solution to overcome this obstacle? The same as for excuse number two. How involved are you in the mission work itself?

Excuse Number Four:
"I'M AFRAID TO FLY"

A good friend of John's once shared with him a story of his being on an airplane. He found himself seated next to a non-believer. As they talked, the non-believer asked him about his faith and he shared how Jesus has made a difference in his life. The conversation continued with the non-believer showing more and more interest. The non-believer said John's friend's faith seemed very genuine and he truly must have a great relationship with God. Then the weather turned violent and the plane lost considerable altitude. The friend told John he was quite frightened. He held the arms of his seat with white knuckles. In a short time the plane leveled off and all was well. Upon their landing, John's friend asked the non-believer if he could have his card so they could talk some more. The non-believer responded, "No thanks. I learned what you really believe when the plane took a dive".

What a great lesson he learned. First off, if we truly believe in our salvation, the fear of death has to leave our set of emotions. If we really believe God is in charge, then we have nothing to fear. If He allows the plane we're on to crash, then we know He will use that for good somehow. From His perspective it will turn out fine. Being a professional speaker, John flies over 100,000 miles each year. He figures if there is plane trouble he can't lose. If there is a crash and he is killed he knows where he is going, if he survives he has a great story to tell.

Please understand that some people can think of the above but still experience fear. That is because they have held the belief so long or so emotionally that it is virtually automatic and defies logic. As a certified hypnotherapist, John has helped many people overcome the fear of flying. It is just a matter of breaking the unconscious connections that trigger the response. If this is a real fear for you and not an excuse, we can help you overcome it as part of your training.

In addition, if this is your excuse you should be very concerned about your faith and relationship with the Lord.

Is there any faith without some risk? Is there any faith without obeying the Lord's call? Are you instead trusting in yourself more than you trust in the Lord?

Excuse Number Five:
"LET THE PROS DO IT"

The person who uses this excuse is saying that world missions is the job of church leaders. They have spectator status in the church. They have paid their price of admission, so now they are entitled to sit in the pews and watch what their money has bought. It's like buying a ticket to an NBA game. You now have the right to watch the professionals play basketball. The local team would never let you on the court to start playing the game with them. Those who use this excuse assume it's the same with the church. Sit back and watch the pros do it. They can do missions better than you, right? Why should anyone expect you to get involved? Just pay the pros to do it.

Remember how at the beginning of the book we mentioned that God involves us in missions because He wants to share the joy and experience with us. Sure a professional could do it better, but God didn't want you to miss out on the experience and the blessing. Don't be fooled like some who believe the Bible's teaching, "...to go to all the nations," only applies to a few people in the church, certainly not to every follower of Jesus.

Most of these people do not even pay attention to what God is doing in the world. Over 100,000 Christians are being martyred every year around the world. Over 70,000 people around the world are coming to faith in Jesus each day. Who cares? It's a game the pros are playing across the sea. Let them handle it.

The secret to overcoming this excuse is to understand the true nature of the Great Commission. When you realize it applies to every Christian, you know you need to be a part of the team. You realize there is a place for the professional, but there is also a place for you.

Excuse Number Six:
"OUR YOUTH GO TO MEXICO EVERY YEAR"

Here we go again. The myth that I am immune to the call because I am already involved. This time I get credit because my children or the children of my friends at church are going on the mission and after all I bought cookies at the bake sale so I am involved. As with the previous two excuses, the key question is how involved are you? Are you truly a sender or a pretender?

Excuse Number Seven:
"I WOULD HAVE DONE THAT WHEN I WAS YOUNGER, BUT I'M RETIRED NOW."

This is an exciting one from our perspective. No matter what your age, you are only as old as you perceive yourself. Even as we wrote the notes for this chapter there was a gentleman sitting two rows behind me who is 94 years young. I am greeted many Sundays by Ray who at age 69 went on a mission to Kenya with his 41 year old son, Rob.

If you feel old, you need a reason to stay young. Going a mission for God can help make you feel younger. Once again, there is no ache, pain, or disability with which God can't work. Even death isn't a disabling injury in God's workplace.

There is absolutely no concept of retirement for a Christian in the Bible. So many Americans have come to the conclusion they will only be productive for a certain number of years. At some point, they have "earned the right" to relax and do what they want. From God's perspective, if you have reached retirement you now have more time to develop your relationship with Him. This does not mean those of you who haven't retired should put it off.

What a terrible misconception to have invaded the church of Jesus Christ. For us, who are followers of Jesus, we are given the joy and the honor to proclaim God's glory to all the peoples of the world until our dying breath. What could be worse than to be taken out of the game and be made a spectator? People in their 60's, 70's, and sometimes even people in their 80's are very capable of being missionaries to the nations, whether for a couple of weeks or a few years. We have already witnessed the outstanding ministry of some retired people who do not use this excuse to stay home and do nothing.

Do you have to be in perfect health to be a missionary? Of course not. When people see you coming to them with a few aches and pains, or a bit of a limp, they are even more ready to listen to you. They wonder, why would you bother with them, when you could have stayed on your comfortable couch far away? What is so important to move you to go share with them, in spite of your discomfort? Indeed, they are ready to listen.

If you are concerned whether you have what it takes to go on a mission you are in luck. That is one of the jobs of *The Sending Place*™. We will help you evaluate your situation and find a mission in which you can work. If not, let us tell you so you know it isn't just an excuse.

Excuse Number Eight:
"I CAN'T AFFORD IT, AND I CAN'T ASK OTHERS FOR MONEY"

This is a good example of how we tend to use language to keep us in a stuck state. This excuse is actually saying, "I can't afford it, and I don't want to ask others for money." I don't know your personal finances, but let's assume you don't have the personal funds to go. This can actually be a good thing. This gives you the opportunity to allow others to become senders. They will be able to be actively involved in God's Great Commission. They get to get off the bench and help you go. They might even be led to go when they hear your reports of how it benefited your life.

The danger of this excuse is that it actually weakens your faith and relationship with God. This excuse shows a complete trust of yourself, to the exclusion of trusting the Lord. This excuse is one satan uses by disguising it as a seemingly positive trait -- that we are self-reliant and can take care of ourselves. They do not want to depend on anyone for anything. What they cannot afford, they will not do.

We need to remember that even Jesus and His disciples were able to do ministry because other people donated money for their livelihood. Luke 8:3 refers to the women "...who provided for them out of their means."

Sometimes this excuse is really about fear of being rejected. They do not want to take the risk of being rejected by asking others for help.

This, like other excuses, has much to do with being honest with ourselves. If we are honest, we are creating the illusion we are strong and independent. But the reality is we are becoming stuck in a small world. Trusting the Lord to help us accomplish great things beyond our own ability is where we show true strength. Whenever we trust in God, we grow stronger and our faith is strengthened.

Excuse Number Nine:
"MY CHILDREN ARE TOO YOUNG"

As we mentioned earlier, the key is to be honest with ourselves and with God. This can be a very valid reason, or just another excuse. It truly is difficult to leave very small children for two or three weeks to serve on a mission team. Some take their children along, but that can be a distraction for the rest of the team, and it can be difficult for those children to see and experience some of the dramatic sights.

The question becomes, when does this "reason" become an "excuse?" At some age, children are certainly old enough to go along, and handle most situations that arise. At some age, they are also old enough to leave at home in the care of a responsible family member or friend. Each parent must be honest, look deep inside, and determine whether this is an excuse or a good reason.

If this is a real reason, then jump off the bench and onto the field to serve as a sender. More importantly, pick a date when you believe your children will be old enough for you to leave them for a short mission. Put it on your calendar. Contact us and let us know. We can begin to prepare you. This will make it a real commitment instead of an excuse. Someday is not a date, and people who say they will do something "someday," very seldom get around to it.

Excuse Number Ten:
"WE HAVE SO MANY PROGRAMS IN OUR CHURCH RIGHT NOW, WE JUST DON'T HAVE TIME FOR ANY MORE."

This excuse prevents people from actually energizing their congregation to accomplish even more than they do now. Taking part in world missions stretches the vision of a congregation, which in turn creates greater involvement of more members, which in turn brings more people to the team to get the work done.

The larger the congregation, the more dangerous this excuse becomes. As a congregation tries to meet the needs of its members, the church calendar fills with meetings, studies, support groups, and fellowship. As members seek to fulfill "what's in it for me," reaching out to the world can be forgotten, even though we may speak or sing about it often.

After hearing a singer perform a beautiful rendition of a song which spoke about going to the nations to proclaim God's word, we later asked the singer when she would like to go on a mission team. The stuttering and stammering that followed was quite sad. We completely took her by surprise. She knew that song by memory, but had never thought of actually doing what it proclaimed!

As we mentioned earlier, if meeting the needs of the local congregation is a legitimate concern instead of an excuse, the solution is to become involved in missions. God strengthens churches that are outwardly focused. If you want to truly accomplish great things in your community, church, home, and family you need to embrace world missions personally.

Excuse Number Eleven:
"WE'RE DOING A BIG BUILDING PROJECT RIGHT NOW, AND CANNOT AFFORD TO DO ANYTHING ELSE"

This is virtually the same as the previous excuse. The reality is the expansion of world missions will inevitably increase activity and giving because of the excitement caused by those who send and go.

Building projects require lots of time, money, and energy. Constant meetings eat up your evenings, stewardship campaigns stretch your financial resources, and all the concerns about details, setbacks, and deadlines are exhausting. As Senior Pastor, Darrel has been a leader in four major building projects. These issues are real. Do not allow them to be excuses for neglecting to keep working on The Great Commission that Jesus has called us to do. Your returning short-term missionaries will give your congregation renewed vision to complete the work at home and abroad.

Excuse Number Twelve:
"WE'RE ALREADY SUPPORTING SEVERAL MISSIONARIES"

While supporting full time missionaries is a necessary and wonderful thing, sometimes a little support is a dangerous thing. Sometimes a congregation will send $2,000 or $3,000 to a few different missionaries, and think they have done all that is necessary for world missions. It may be an infinitesimally small part of the church's budget, but it is considered enough. One question you need to ask is, how much has your support of missions in your budget increased every year? If it hasn't grown, then it has actually gone backwards. Because of inflation, the dollar buys less every year. Now would be a good time to increase the growth of missions by continuing to support your current mission commitments and join in the support of short-term missions. Supporting *The Sending Place*™ is a great opportunity to do this.

If this is used as an excuse it actually limits your church by not allowing individuals to actually go. It is exciting to see what can happen when those who have actually gone on a mission are in your church every Sunday sharing their enthusiasm with their fellow members and guests. Don't let yourself and your church be cheated out of this great experience.

Excuse Number Thirteen:
"WE SUPPORT (SOME OTHER AGENCY)"
Once again, this is similar to the preceding excuse. Growth is achieved by stretching. We encourage you to evaluate what you think God can provide and step out in faith to reach more people around the world.

The Sending Place™ is a unique Missionary Training Center. We are not in competition with anyone else, because no one else is doing exactly what we are doing. This excuse can be used to justify to themselves they are already doing enough for world missions. They give a few dollars to another mission agency, so no more involvement is necessary. They are now off the hook.

Excuse Number Fourteen:
"WE JUST WANT TO EASE INTO MISSIONS. MAYBE WE'LL CALL YOU LATER"
This is an illusion or a trick satan uses to delay and eventually prevent us from being involved in missions. If your house were burning down would you ease into putting it out? Of course not. Who could face someone saying to them, "We can't share the eternal life-giving Gospel with you because we are just going to ease into it. Maybe we will get to your village to save your children someday".

The real way to grow your faith and the faith of your congregation is to step out knowing the Lord will provide. Easing into something is the way we do it when we are trusting in ourselves not in God. God doesn't need to ease into anything. He can get it done for you when you let Him.

The illusion works. Planning on doing it feels like you are involved, which means you don't have to do anything else. If this is your excuse, are you fooling yourself into thinking you are involved in missions because you intend to do something later? The reality is, they usually never quite get around to it. Later never comes.

Excuse Number Fifteen:
"I KNOW OF ANOTHER GROUP DOING MISSION WORK. WHY DON'T YOU CONTACT THEM?"

This is another illusion that keeps us uninvolved. We trick ourselves into thinking we are helping by offering advice. Believe us, advice is everywhere. It is work and action that makes things happen. This excuse seems to justify in the speaker's mind they have somehow helped ours or any other ministry, somehow been involved in the task of missions, even though they have done absolutely nothing themselves. That other mission group is doing good work. *The Sending Place*™ is doing good work. Why don't we just get together, and everything will be fine. Now leave me alone. The church is a body made up of many parts. God doesn't want to merge all these parts into one part. Each accomplishes what it does well, just as the parts of our body do. Thank goodness your brain doesn't buy this excuse or it might cut off the blood supply to any body part that chooses not to merge with the others.

SOME CONCLUDING THOUGHTS

We often wonder when we choose to ignore something we know God wants us to do, if it tells us something about what we really believe. If we really believed the most powerful being in the universe asked us to do something, it seems unlikely we would defy him. On the other hand, we can fool ourselves into thinking He isn't talking to us, or we are the exception to the rule.

Remember to trust God; look into your own heart. If an obstacle is not an excuse, then you and God are actively breaking through it. When it comes to reaching the people of the world, you can rest assured God would not allow an obstacle to hold you back if you trusted it to Him and went ahead in spite of it.

Chapter 11

What We Have Left Undone

"As we seek to find out why, with such millions of Christians, the real army of God that is fighting the hosts of darkness is so small, the only answer is—lack of heart. The enthusiasm of the kingdom is missing. And that is because there is so little enthusiasm for the King."

--Andrew Murray

Questions To Enhance Your Reading

1. What is my place in the Great Commission?

2. What of God's work have I left undone, distracted by other things?

3. What have I left undone this week that God wanted me to do?

4. Who did I declare the Glory of God to this week?

WHAT WE HAVE LEFT UNDONE

I, Darrel, and my wife live in a home surrounded by 5 acres of property. There is a red barn with white trim in the center of the property, right in the middle of a fence that goes down the center of our land. The front half of our property is where we built our home, which is surrounded by lots of lawn, and a circular driveway which has 36 roses inside the circle, which are really quite beautiful most of the year. We have also planted well over 100 trees around and inside our place. We have lots of fruit trees and grape vines, too.

It's a lot of work to keep the place looking good. Lots of mowing, pruning, spraying, and weeding is required. When I became director of *The Sending Place*™, I did a great deal of traveling. Being on the road caused a lot of work to be left undone. For the first time, I did not get the pruning finished this spring. A few months ago, we had a major wind storm which blew over three trees, and I still have not gotten around to cutting them up. We started painting the outside of our house two years ago, and we still have not finished part of it on the back side.

What about you? Are there chores around your house which you have left undone? Are there tasks at your work which you have left unfinished? Are there projects at school whose deadlines are approaching, but they are still not done?

Even more importantly, are there vital things in your life that you have left undone? There is an interesting phrase in some of the Lutheran hymnals in the corporate confession of sin at the beginning of the worship liturgy, where the worshipper asks God to forgive us for "what we have left undone." We have a hunch the vast majority of people who say this confession of sin spend very little time thinking about the specific things they have left undone, which are sins to be confessed.

Have you spent much time pondering those things God has called you to do, but which you continue, day after day, week after week, year after year, to leave undone? Think about it for a moment right now. What have you left undone this week that God wanted you to do? Go ahead...think!

What did you think about? Maybe you thought about how you did not tell your spouse you loved them. Maybe you thought about that letter you were going to write to your mom or dad. Perhaps you thought about that project at work you did not get around to. Perhaps you thought about that school homework project you should have started by now. Maybe you did not pray very much this week, or missed going to Bible Study. Perhaps you sat by and watched someone be mistreated.

Maybe your mind was blank. You could not think of a thing that you left undone, which God called you to do. Actually, that is probably pretty common.

Try this little exercise, which can reveal a lot. If you are having trouble thinking of some, try to develop a list of things you didn't get done this week that you or your family wanted you to do. Things like cleaning the garage, repairing a chair, fixing a sprinkler on the lawn, etc. If it is easy to come up with a list of earthly things that you have left undone but not easy to come up with a list of what you have left undone for God, it could mean one of two things. First, you are a saint and are serving God so much that you get everything done He asks of you, or more likely you are focused on the things of the world more than the things of God. The closer our relationship with God is the more we will become aware of two lists. First, what God has accomplished with our life, the things we have done which give glory to Him. Second, the things we have left undone. Now try the list again and take a moment to write down a few.

_____

_____

_____

_____

_____

If you take time to ponder the sins you have done and the things you have left undone, we bet the vast majority of us rarely think about even one specific thing we have not done. We only think of a few blunders we made, that we regret doing or saying, and focus on those.

We believe our greatest sins in the eyes of God could very well come from the category that we rarely even think about—those things we have left undone! In the Bible, the book of James covers this subject extensively. James 2:17 says, "Faith by itself, if it has no works, is dead." And James 4:17 concludes, "Whoever knows what is right to do and fails to do it, for him it is sin."

Many people might think they had a good day if they did not swear, did not get angry, and did not offend anyone. James makes it clear. You can sit home and do absolutely nothing to hurt anyone, and still be sinning greatly, because you are leaving crucial things undone!

We Have Left the Biggest Thing of all Undone

There are many things that we could talk about in this category, but right in this chapter we just want to discuss the biggest thing of all. We believe that we in the church of Jesus Christ, we who call ourselves followers of Jesus, have left the most important task of all undone! And most of us go our merry way, giving it no thought whatsoever.

What is this big thing we have left undone? In Acts 1:8 Jesus gives some very important instructions to His disciples and tells them, "You shall be my witnesses in Jerusalem, and in all Judea and Samaria and to the end of the earth." He also says in Matthew 28:18-19, "All authority in heaven and on earth has been given to me. Go therefore and make disciples of all nations." This isn't shared with His followers as an afterthought! Jesus was giving them their marching orders so they would know what their tasks were when He was gone.

In the church, we refer to this as evangelism and missions. Evangelism is declaring Jesus to the people nearby, in your community, your neighborhoods, your school, and your workplace, many of whom you already know. Missions is declaring Jesus to the people far away, people you probably don't know. Most of us in the Christian community in this country are leaving evangelism and missions hugely undone!

What about you? Who did you declare the glory of God to this week? Where are you preparing to go overseas to preach and teach that Gospel, or who are you helping to send to do that task overseas?

If you did no evangelism this week, and you did not focus on world missions this week, you have fallen into the sin of leaving the things of God undone. When you pray for forgiveness for the things you have left undone, make sure this comes to mind immediately! But then, don't just feel guilty about leaving it undone, while you continue to leave it undone.

Begin more and more to live out Jesus' call for us to do evangelism and missions! Take seriously the words of Psalm 96:2-3, as you "tell of his salvation from day to day. Declare his glory among the nations, his marvelous works among all the peoples."

Sadly our most important task commissioned by Jesus Himself is the one we leave undone more than any other one! We have left it undone for far too long. It's time to get on with actually living out this joy and this honor, of showing God's name and fame and reputation to all nations!

The Greatest Mission Activity of All Time is Now

Most all missionaries and mission agencies we talk to are in complete agreement on one thing: Right now, God is busy doing the greatest mission activity of all time! Some statistics we were given in a class called "Perspectives On the World Christian Movement" were astonishing. It is estimated that 70,000 new believers are coming to Christ every day throughout the world! 28,000 of those new believers each day are in China! Another 20,000 of those new believers are in Africa. Throughout the world, there are 3,500 new churches starting each week. This is exciting stuff. We get the impression sitting here at home that Christianity is on the decline. It may be where you live but we suspect it is only because we have not paid attention to Jesus' last directive. For much of creation if something isn't growing it is dying. This is certainly true of the church. If you want your local church to grow you must be involved in missions that go beyond your world.

God is on the move, using His people to do wonderful things! But do you know where there is an exception to this? Can you name one of the few countries of the world where the Christian church is not growing? I hate to say it, but it's right here in the United States. Amidst the greatest mission activity of all time, most Americans seem more interested in what is on television tonight, than how they can be a goer or sender for the Lord. The sad truth is that much of this lack of growth comes from looking inward instead of outward. What do we mean by this? For too many years we have been focused on fixing our social hall, the new kitchen, stained glass windows and the like. Not that any of these things are bad. The trick is that we begin to focus on ourselves even though we think we are doing it for God. As we struggle to raise a few dollars for a worthy building project, we begin to think how we can cut back on the budget for next year since giving seems to be down. It is a slippery slope. As we cut back, our vision shrinks and we cut back some more. So what is the solution? Trust God with a greater mission. Commit to getting done the work He called us to do and the rest will seem easy. A church that is focused outward will grow, and the funds and resources it needs will be there. When you have a congregation of those who have been actively involved in changing the world they easily find the resources to provide for the local needs of the congregation. They also attract others which helps their church grow.

Right in the middle of God's incredible mission activity, this is not the time to be content to be a spectator! It's time we jump into the battle, time to jump onto the field—the mission field, that is. As Henry T. Blackaby says in his book <u>Experiencing God</u>, "When I see the Father at work around me, that is my invitation to adjust my life to Him and join Him in that work."

Are You Ready?

Are you ready for a life of greater fulfillment? Are you ready for a life of greater adventure? Are you ready to join in and be part of God's great mission activity? We would love to help you accomplish this. Contact us at *The Sending Place*™, and let us help you get moving on what you have left undone. Pick up the phone right now and call us at 877-3-SENDING or 916-685-2331

Chapter 12

God Is A Missionary God

"But how are men to call upon him in whom they have not believed? And how are they to believe in him of whom they have never heard? And how are they to hear without a preacher? And how can men preach unless they are sent? As it is written, 'How beautiful are the feet of those who preach good news!' "

-- Romans 10:14-15

Questions To Enhance Your Reading

1. What is my place in the Great Commission?

2. What is faith?

3. Is missions some new idea that God recently thought of?

4. How many people does God want to be in heaven?

God Called His People To Go From The Beginning

God's call to His followers to GO and proclaim His word to all the peoples of the earth is not new! Long before Paul did it, long before Jesus proclaimed it, God told His people throughout Old Testament history that He wanted ALL peoples to give Him glory! It began in Genesis 12:1-3, where God called Abraham to become the father of a new nation, which would ultimately be a blessing to **ALL** the families of the earth. God told him, "I will bless those who bless you, and him who curses you I will curse; and by you all the families of the earth shall bless themselves." God does not want to be the Lord of just a few people, He wants to be Lord of ALL peoples! Although the nation of Israel never really embraced this concept, they sang about it frequently in their Psalms. Psalm 22:27 says, "All the ends of the earth shall remember and turn to the Lord; and all the families of the nations shall worship before him." But they didn't take any action that would lead other people and nations to give glory to the one true God.

What joyful singing can be heard in Psalm 67:4 "Let the nations be glad and sing for joy, for you judge the people with equity and guide the nations upon earth." And Psalm 96:2-3 certainly seems clear as to what the Lord expects of His people, "Tell of his salvation from day to day. Declare his glory among the nations, his marvelous works among all the peoples!"

But even after singing about God being a missionary God, wanting all peoples to give Him glory, the nation of Israel continued to ignore Him. They seemed to want to keep God to themselves. Sadly in similar fashion, many people in churches today want to remain small and comfortable without having to deal with growth that would come from following God's Great Commission. God didn't create a private club just for us, He wants to include everyone.

When Jesus came to the earth, He frequently taught the same missionary mandate to those who would become His followers. In the famous Sermon on the Mount, Jesus proclaimed in Matthew 5:14 and 16, "You are the light of the world...Let your light so shine before men, that they may see your good works and give glory to your Father who is in heaven."

The Great Commission

This book has already quoted Jesus a number of times when He gives us the Great Commission in Matthew 28:19-20, that what we are to be doing after Jesus conquered sin and death for us is to "Go therefore and make disciples of all nations, baptizing them in the name of the Father and of the Son and of the Holy Spirit, teaching them to observe all that I have commanded you; and lo, I am with you always, to the close of the age."

Over and over, Jesus and His early disciples tried to motivate Jesus' followers to take seriously this task of being missionaries to the ends of the earth. But in many ways, the modern Christian Church in the past has ignored this mandate, almost as much as the nation of Israel did in the Old Testament.

Today Is An Exciting Time

The exciting fact is that perhaps now more than any time in recent history more and more people and churches are responding to God's Great Commission. Missions and those who go and send are on the increase. This means you have the opportunity to join God in what may be the greatest spread of the Gospel since the first generation of Christians was on fire for the Lord. It may be possible that you're coming into contact with this book and ministry is another invitation God is giving you to become involved.

The Sending Place™ has been called by God to recruit, train, and send more and more of God's people to not only accept this fact that God is a missionary God, but to put it into action by becoming His missionaries themselves! God has inspired us and taught us through our experience and that of others how to help you be faithful and successful in responding to God's calling.

Acts 4:12 is clear when it says, "There is salvation in no one else, for there is no other name (Jesus) under heaven given among men by which we must be saved." Jesus is the only door into the kingdom of heaven. And He has promised that there will be someone from every group of people in the world, who will accept faith in the Lord Jesus Christ, and be found in heaven! Isn't that exciting to you? Just think, as a short-term missionary, you can help spread that word to all kinds of people. You can get to know Christians from all kinds of races and cultures. You will know more people in heaven than you ever dreamed!

You can share the Lord's excitement in the kingdom of heaven, when He looks around and sees what He promises us in Revelation 7:9-10, "After this I looked, and behold, a great multitude which no man could number, from every nation, from all tribes and peoples and tongues, standing before the throne and before the Lamb, clothed in white robes, with palm branches in their hands, and crying out with a loud voice, 'Salvation belongs to our God who sits upon the throne, and to the Lamb!' " How wonderful to be a part of that throng knowing many of those around you were introduced to God through your missionary efforts.

God is indeed a missionary God, always calling us to be a missionary people.

Chapter 13

What Is My Next Step?

"Putting your faith into action is what makes things happen."
-- John W. Drebinger Jr.

Questions To Enhance Your Reading

1. What is my place in the Great Commission?

2. What am I really willing to do next to get personally involved in world missions?

3. Am I ready to be a "Goer" for the Lord? Or Am I going to take seriously the task of being a "Sender" for those who are willing to go?

4. What can my congregation do to get everyone personally involved in missions?

Take Action!

You're now convinced. You understand better than ever before that God is a missionary God, who wants all peoples to be in His kingdom through faith in Jesus Christ. So what do you do now? Whether you are called to be a sender or a goer the next step is the same. Are you near a phone, or do you use email? In either case contact, us <u>right</u> <u>now</u>! You can call us 24 hours a day at 877-3-SENDING or 916-685-2331 or email us at <u>director@thesendingplace.com</u> . The reason we want you to do this is that action is important at this stage of the game! It is very easy to feel committed and let that substitute for real action. By calling or contacting us you know you have actually entered the mission field as we will help you keep going. Putting your faith into action is what makes things happen, so take action now before you read any further and contact us.

Now you have taken the first step - what happens next? First we need to know what you sense God is calling you to do. Are you ready to be a "Goer?" That is, are you willing to take some risks because you love the Lord and are willing to do the greatest work of all? Are you ready to step out of your personal comfort zone, train with *The Sending Place*™, fly across the ocean, and let God use you for His glory, to spread His fame to others? If so, when we talk to you we will ask you to fill out a registration form! You can do so by mail, by phone, or e-mail. If you want more information, look at our website at: www.thesendingplace.com.

Get Some Training

Training begins in August for mission teams going overseas during the winter months, while training begins in January for those teams going forth during the summer. If you don't yet have a passport, go to your local post office, pick up the form, and begin the process of getting your passport. Find a place in town that takes passport photos (some post offices can do this on site), fill out the form, and make an appointment back at the post office to make your application.

Read All Training Materials

Next, when the day arrives for your training to begin through *The Sending Place*™, come with the determination that you will study all the materials, and read all of the assigned books, so you can be the best-trained missionary you can possibly be! The training will walk you through what you need to know to make your mission trip be a successful adventure, so don't worry about what you don't yet know concerning the place you have chosen to go, or all the details of ministry you will be doing. Relax, and go with the training. You'll be fine. You're about to experience more adventure and fulfillment than you probably ever have before!

Become A Sender

If you are not a "Goer" at this time, then you are a "Sender". We want to help you become the best "Sender" you can possibly be. If you are ready to become a serious "Sender", you will start setting money aside to make that happen. When the "Goers" from your congregation begin raising the finances that are needed, you'll be ready to respond.

I know a growing number of people who are serious about being good senders. As a part of their regular tithe to God's work, they donate monthly to the general fund of *The Sending Place*™. They also have developed a system to help the individual goers when the need arises. They do this by setting aside additional funds in their bank account that they hold in reserve. When the goers send out their letters asking for financial support, the senders are ready to respond with the funds in that reserve.

In 2004 a short-term mission trip can cost $3,000, $4,000 or more, depending on how far they will travel. (The major cost of a mission trip is the airline ticket and training.) Here is a good place to explain that the role of a sender is much more than financial support. In fact we encourage our "goers" to always raise the support for their mission because we want them to build a team that is part of that mission. Even if they have the personal resources to pay for the trip themselves, that would leave them all alone when they leave to go on their mission. Instead, by gathering the financial support, they are expanding the mission field by including senders like you in their outreach to the world.

Involve Your Home Congregation

We have found some of the best impact a goer can have is when they are able to involve their own congregation. If your congregation does not yet have a "Mission Fund" established for the purpose of sending short-term missionaries, it is time to get such a fund established immediately. As a sender, you can multiply your effectiveness when you get your congregation involved in missions this way. By setting up such a fund, the congregation is making it clear that from now on, they are going to be personally involved in the task of world missions, and will support all their members to do so.

As the finances are being raised by the "Goers", the 'Senders' will take the task of prayer very seriously. *The Sending Place*™ will not let anyone train or go overseas who does not have a considerable number of prayer partners who are daily keeping the missionary and their family in prayer.

Remember, the devil does not want any of these missionaries to go preach or teach the Gospel of Jesus Christ. He will begin almost immediately to distract or side-track the missionary from going overseas. Your job as a good "Sender" is to cover that missionary with daily prayer, during training as well as on the mission trip.

We have witnessed a lot of healing and protection the Lord has given these missionaries, and it all came about through the faithful prayers of God's faithful people, the "Senders."

As training proceeds, the "Goers" will continue to need your on-going support and encouragement. It is amazing how many so-called "well meaning" Christians and relatives will keep trying to talk the missionary out of going! After all, there is risk involved, and they're going so far from home, and what about the terrorists in the world, and so on and so on. In addition, some people are discouraging others because it makes them feel uncomfortable that they haven't accepted God's call to either be a sender or a goer themselves.

Some of that can shake up the "Goer." It's up to you to be an encourager, reminding them of such promises from scripture as Matthew 28:20, where Jesus makes it clear, that as you do go and work at making disciples of all the nations, "I am with you ALWAYS, to the close of the age."

Remind them of the wonderful promise of Philippians 4:6-7, "Have no anxiety about anything, but in everything by prayer and supplication with thanksgiving let your requests be made known to God. And the peace of God, which passes all understanding, will keep your hearts and your minds in Christ Jesus."

Matthew 6:33-34 is also a great passage of encouragement to remind the "Goer," "Seek first his kingdom and his righteousness, and all these things shall be yours as well. Therefore do not be anxious about tomorrow, for tomorrow will be anxious for itself."

The missionaries might also need a variety of supplies that are needed for their particular mission. Office supplies, school supplies, medical supplies, extra luggage, Christian coloring books and many other things could be needed. Good "Senders" can also provide many of these items, when the needs are announced.

After the trip is over, a good "Sender" will actually want to know about what happened on the mission trip, ask how the trip went, and actively listen to what they want to share about their experience. We have discovered that it is very difficult for a missionary to return with a high level of excitement only to be met by disinterest. They love you for helping them achieve what was done on their mission, and afterwards they want you to be a part of the success and joy. When you share their joy and excitement you will affect the missionary and they will love and appreciate you like you cannot imagine!

We also encourage the sending congregations to have a number of events centered on the missionary journey. That day will come when the "Goers" must head for the airport. A congregational "send-off" is a wonderful event for everyone! We encourage a brief time of worship, perhaps with Holy Communion, and then have all the "Senders" gather around the "Goers" for a time of prayer. Such support is a very powerful emotional and spiritual lift for the missionaries as they leave on their mission!

While the missionaries are away, we encourage the sending congregations to have evening prayer gatherings every day for the mission team and for the people to which they are ministering. As the team sends e-mails with what is happening, interest is high at home. Special needs may become known, such as when a missionary may be ill. We have witnessed some of those missionaries being healed at the exact time they were being prayed for by their "Senders" back home! Indeed, good "Senders" are a powerful force for the "Goers."

The time when the mission team returns home is also a very special moment, worthy of having a "welcome home" gathering in the church parking lot. The mood is very different from the send-off, when the missionaries left with high enthusiasm and some degree of anxiety. The welcome home is much more subdued, as the missionaries return very tired, and often feeling rather overwhelmed by what they have just experienced. It takes a few days for their "jet lag" to diminish. Continue to pray for them and support them.

Report To Your Congregation

There is one more event that is crucial at the congregational level. It is very important to allow the missionaries some time to give a report to the congregation on a Sunday morning. Perhaps, a brief temple talk at each worship service, which also points members to the Sunday School hour when the missionaries give their full report. Pictures or power point presentations are often used to bring the adventure to life for the congregation. This is a powerful moment when many "Senders" come to the personal realization "I can do that!"

This is the approach that was used at St. Peter's Lutheran Church in Elk Grove, California, where this Missionary Training Center had its first beginnings. In its first year of involvement, the congregation sent out one adult on an overseas, short-term mission trip. The second year, a few more were added. By the fifth year, over 20 adults went overseas on short-term mission trips! We went from one to twenty in just five years. Could that happen in your congregation? If it did, how do you think that would change the ministry and focus of your church? How many missionaries might be going overseas after ten years? Will you be among them?

Collection of
Empowering Quotes

"Committing your thoughts to print creates a void in your mind which your creative spirit will fill with new ideas"
-- John W. Drebinger Jr.

"Writing down your ideas, questions, and commitments is like planting them in fertile soil."
- John W. Drebinger Jr.

"Expect great things from God. Attempt great things for God."
-William Carey

"It's one of the greatest joys of a short-term mission—seeing God break down barriers that separate us. We get to taste what heaven will be like—to know hints of the joy of Pentecost, to glimpse our gathering before the throne of God."
-- J. Mack and Leeann Stiles

"God doesn't need you to reach the world for Christ, He can do it on His own, but why would you want to miss out on the joy?"
--John W. Drebinger Jr.

"The difficulty or challenge of a problem is gauged by your viewpoint. Looking at it from our perspective, it may appear overwhelming, but from God's perspective it's much smaller and achievable."
-- John W. Drebinger Jr.

"So many people today merely exist while living a life filled only with trivia."
--Darrel Deuel

"Only by being there and feeling and smelling for themselves will they understand the need."
-- George Verwer

"The great news is that short-term missions open up the mission field to 'ordinary people'. I hope you can see yourself as part of that wave"

-- Darrel Deuel

"Everyone has faith, the question is; where do you put your faith, into action?"

-- John Drebinger

"If we don't adopt a commitment to excellence in our missionary thrust, I believe that we are going to be laying up big problems for ourselves in the future."

--George Verwer

"What I want to tell you is that the team, you, *The Sending Place*™, sent here was the best team we have ever had—bar none! They came to do a job and went about doing it without any fuss, confusion, or problems. And how wonderfully they represented the Lord."

--Nita Hanson

"As we began to gear up toward sending our own teams on short-term mission trips we wanted to be sure they had the proper training to make the mission a success for them and those they went to serve"

-- Darrel Deuel

"We measure the worth of a hidden treasure by what we will gladly sell to buy it. If we will sell all, then we measure the worth as supreme. If we will not, what we have is treasured more."

--John Piper

"As we seek to find out why, with such millions of Christians, the real army of God that is fighting the hosts of darkness is so small, the only answer is—lack of heart. The enthusiasm of the kingdom is missing. And that is because there is so little enthusiasm for the King."

--Andrew Murray

"But how are men to call upon him in whom they have not believed? And how are they to believe in him of whom they have never heard? And how are they to hear without a preacher? And how can men preach unless they are sent? As it is written, 'How beautiful are the feet of those who preach good news!' "

-- Romans 10:14-15

"Putting your faith into action is what makes things happen."

-- John W. Drebinger Jr.

Idea Journal

Thoughts and ideas from reading …
What is my place in the Great Commission?

Thoughts and ideas from reading ...
What is my place in the Great Commission?

Thoughts and ideas from reading...
What is my place in the Great Commission?

Thoughts and ideas from reading …
What is my place in the Great Commission?

Recommended Reading List

Davey, Cyril. **On The Clouds to China, The Story of Hudson Taylor.** Guildford, Surrey: Lutterworth Press, 1964

DeVries, Dr. John F. **Does It Pay to Pray?**. Grand Rapids, Michigan: Mission India, 1998

Murray, Andrew. **The Key to the Missionary Problem**. Fort Washington, Pennsylvania: Christian Literature Crusade, 1979

Olson, Bruce. **Bruchko**. Lake Mary, Florida: Charisma House, 1995

Piper, John. **Let the Nations Be Glad.** Grand Rapids, Michigan: Baker Academic, 2003

Pirolo, Neal. **Serving as Senders**. San Diego, California: Emmaus Road, International, 1991

Schlink, M. Basilea. **Allah or the God of the Bible—What is the Truth?** Darmstadt, Germany: Evangelical Sisterhood of Mary, 1984

Stiles, J. Mack & Leeann. **Mack & Leeann's Guide to Short-Term Missions**. Downers Grove, Illinois: InterVarsity Press, 2000

Telford, Tom. **Today's All-Star Missions Churches**. Grand Rapids, Michigan: Baker Books, 2001

Verwer, George. **Out of the Comfort Zone**. Mosbach, Germany: Operation Mobilisation, 2000

Winter, Ralph D. (U.S. Center for World Mission. **Vision for the Nations**. Pasadena, California: William Carey Library, 1995

Winter, Ralph D. and Hawthorne, Steven C. **Perspectives on the World Christian Movement**. Pasadena, California: William Carey Library, 1999

Yohannan, K.P. **Revolution in World Missions**. Carrollton, Texas: Gospel for Asia, 2002

Pastor Darrel Deuel

Pastor Darrel Deuel grew up on the coast of northern California in the town of Arcata. He was raised in the Lutheran Church there along with his sister, Deanna, thanks to the faithfulness of their parents, Francis and Elina. He has been married to Janet for over 30 years, and they have 3 children, Jamie, Dan, and Darren, and 4 grandchildren, David, Emily, Cody, and Tatum.

He served as a parish pastor for nearly 30 years at two California congregations, St. Timothy's Lutheran Church in San Jose, and St. Peter's Lutheran Church in Elk Grove.

He has had nearly 40 articles and stories published in a variety of magazines, and has had over 100 photos published as well. To get away from the pressures of work and to relax, he enjoys life in the outdoors through hunting, fishing, camping, and photography. He began his call to be full time Executive Director of *The Sending Place*™ in June, 2003. He now travels extensively, preaching about world missions, and recruiting missionaries to be trained by *The Sending Place*™. He trains missionaries, and leads mission teams worldwide.

Phone: 1-916-685-2331
Email: <u>director@thesendingplace.com</u>
Web Site: <u>www.thesendingplace.com</u>

John Warner Drebinger Jr., C.Ht.

John Drebinger works with companies who want communication with results and people who want to give the best presentation their audiences have ever witnessed. He gives people the tools to help them improve their communication skills. His presentations go beyond motivation because they give his audience tools they can put to use immediately to make a difference in their life and the lives of others. He serves a diverse list of clients including, NASA, ExxonMobil, Boeing, Entergy, Shell Oil, ChevronTexaco, Granite Construction, Hunter Douglas, General Mills, United States Air Force, Department of Energy, Bechtel, Haliburton, Tropicana, General Electric, Consolidated Edison, Southern California Edison, IBM, Sony Pictures, and many others. John has a Bachelor's Degree in speech and is a Certified Hypnotherapist. John is a member of the National Speakers Association and he has earned their highest-earned designation, "Certified Speaking Professional."

To contact: John Drebinger Presentations
Toll Free: 1-800-588-9419 Or: 1-209-745-9419
13541 Christensen Rd., Galt, CA, 95632
Email: john@drebinger.com   Web Site: www.drebinger.com

Order Form

$20.00 per copy. Bulk Discounts Available

Fax Orders: (209) 745-4528

Telephone orders: Call Toll Free 1 (800) 588-9419

Have your American Express, Discover, VISA or MasterCard ready.

E-Mail orders: Hypnomagic@drebinger.com

Postal orders: Wulamoc Publishing

13541 Christensen Rd., Suite 200
Galt, CA 95632
Phone: (209) 745-9419

Please send the following items:

Changing The World _____ copies @$20.00 each $_____

Sub Total: $_____

Shipping & Handling: $ _____

Total: $ _____

Name: _____

Address: _____

City:_____ State:_____ Zip:_____

Telephone: (_____) _____

Sales tax: Please add 7.75% for books shipped to California Addresses.

Shipping:

Purchase Total		Add
$0 -------------	$25.00	$3.00
$25.01---------	$100.00.........	$6.00
$100.01-------	$200.00	$10.00
$200.01-------	$300.00	$12.00

Payment:__ Check, Credit Card: ____ VISA, ____ MasterCard ____ AE ____

Discover

Card number: _____

Name on card:_____ Exp. Date: ____ /____

Signature: _____

**Call toll free and order now
1-800-588-9419**

Order Form

$20.00 per copy. Bulk Discounts Available

Fax Orders: (209) 745-4528

Telephone orders: Call Toll Free 1 (800) 588-9419

Have your American Express, Discover, VISA or MasterCard ready.

E-Mail orders: Hypnomagic@drebinger.com

Postal orders: Wulamoc Publishing
                 13541 Christensen Rd., Suite 200
                 Galt, CA 95632
                 Phone: (209) 745-9419

Please send the following items:

Changing The World _____ copies @$20.00 each $_____

Sub Total: $_____

Shipping & Handling: $ _____

Total: $ _____

Name: _____

Address: _____

City:_____ State:_____ Zip:_____

Telephone: (_____) _____

Sales tax: Please add 7.75% for books shipped to California Addresses.

Shipping:	**Purchase Total**		**Add**
	$0 -------------	$25.00	$3.00
	$25.01---------	$100.00.........	$6.00
	$100.01-------	$200.00	$10.00
	$200.01-------	$300.00	$12.00

Payment:__ Check, Credit Card: ____ VISA, ____ MasterCard ____ AE ____

Discover

Card number: _____

Name on card:_____ Exp. Date: ____ /____

Signature: _____

Call toll free and order now
1-800-588-9419